persiawest @ gmail.com

The Choice

REMINDERS TO MYSELF

Persia West

Cover design: Tony Malone
Interior design: Andie Davidson

A CIP catalogue record for this book is available from the British Library.

Published by PersiaWestWords

ISBN 978-0-9572775-0-2

For Janie, of course.

We will have to leave early
at the dawn of your understanding
and risk everything
on love

PW

Introduction

Life around us ebbs and flows, happiness followed by
unhappiness, misery by delight, certainty by distress,
estrangement by love, sweetness by bitterness, on and
on, round and round, or so it seems. It can appear as if
we live a life of dramas that lead nowhere, that we've
read the same life story time after time, day after day,
trapped in a box called 'my life' with no way out. Below
the surface, under our own waterline, there is a great mass
of feelings and thoughts that are the true foundation to
the life we lead and, more often than not, we look
outwards, not inwards, for solution and solace. And so
we keep on chasing our tails, moving ceaselessly but
going nowhere, until we drop.

When the day comes that we want out of this
ongoing drama, when we realise that we'll never catch
the tail—that's when the real journey begins. Everything
begins with intention, so when we really want it, when
we commit to it, when the decision is made once and for
all to get off the merry-go-round, something then moves
within us and a pathway opens, subtly, invisibly, in the
depths of us, and nothing is ever the same again. That is
The Choice.

Contents

1

The Pearl

Like so many people who behave as if they are normal—
because they think it will be a total disaster if they are
real—I pretended for a long, long time to be someone I
wasn't. I created a persona, a mask, to handle so-called
normal life, make me acceptable, loveable, or at least not
rejected and alone. But time passed, and it simply hurt
too much to pretend any more. So one day I threw off the
mask and became myself. It was terrifying to be naked,
without my pretences that made me feel a bit safe in an
apparently normal world. This is because some people
don't like you to be real, to shape-shift in front of them,
maybe because it reminds them of the fragility of their
own pretence, so I was given a hard time by some. I was
given one of the Great Punishments of the social animals
I was part of; I was turned into an outsider, someone who

didn't belong.

At first this was no solution to the conundrum of my life, as it brought a new form of pain. It seemed that I couldn't win either way, keeping my outsider-ness hidden inside or visible outside. But even that got transformed in time, as I found the rich blessings that came with being real to myself and the world around me shifted to meet my honesty. I came to consider my inner pain to be the outer skin of the heart. It is my conviction and experience that if we can penetrate it, live through it, there we find self love.

As time passed, I began to adore that sweet feeling of being myself so much that the passing costs were nothing. It also brought me belonging—anywhere and nowhere, all at the same time. I know that I am that which lies behind any mask I might wear, always for a while. These days I try not to identify as anything at all, unless pressed, or there's some money in it, or if it's useful—as long as I remember not to believe in it and get lost from myself.

I want to share what I've come to know over the years with my sisters and brothers, the black sheep, the outsiders of our world, those whose hearts and natures don't fit within the neat and comfy social boxes of the genders, races, appearances, beliefs and other identities that mean so much to us humans. I want to share my own experience of there being another way to see, that can give us the magic of our own vision, and find a place in this universe that is home, where the heart is.

First of all my dedication, with my love and blessings, to people like me, the gender outlaws, whose gender, the foundation of identity, was assigned at birth and shaped by expectations and rules that were someone else's and were broken, no matter what the price. How blessed we can be when we cross that great inner divide and find ourselves within our longings; how much it can hurt when we don't. My heart goes out to us all, and I hope I can share the way back home, within wisdom and insight, that was given to me.

Then other people, whose nature falls outside the crushing certainties of minds that never considered truth beyond fearful simplicity; women who give light to other women in a million creative ways, nurture and adore each other and meld their bodies in a particular, almost secret fire. Men who love each other with a passion and sweetness incomprehensible to those who love in other ways, in a world of beauty all of their own. Then people whose bodies have more creative genital shapes than most, combining qualities of both male and female and moving beyond them both. All of these delights in colours of identity and being, which are in the nature of our world, our universe. Like the ants and whales and snow leopards in the natural world, the amazing variety of who we are moves beyond the safety of groundless expectation, the tiny ways of mind that want a world, complex beyond our knowing, to be divided clearly into predictable simplicity.

Then, moving wider, we have the countless women of our wide world who feel constrained within the gilded and rusty cages from which their wisdom peers out in perplexed wonder and sadness at the denial of the fullness of their magic being, even by themselves. And all those men who are poets, dreamers and lovers, struggling against the force of expectations that lead them into trenches and nightmares, that emerge with righteousness from someone else's hidden anguish, or those men who find the burden of expectation crushes their own being every working day of their working lives.

Then people even a little different in skin or feature from the expected, or older people, those whose bodies don't function in ways that are expected. And artists and mystics, hermits and yogis, beggars, people who are very tall or big, or smaller than most. Or people who have spiritual ways that are not quite right in the eyes of those who know better, including those like me who have had the delight and wounding of early spiritual revelation, all mixed up with inner and outer identities that seem to contradict each other.

Then everyone else who has at any time in their

lives felt like an outsider, and felt bad or confused about
where they actually belong which, in the end, means just
about every last person in the world. In truth the sense of
separation so many of us feel deep within is, I now see,
nothing other than the loss of our own Self. Maybe,
behind the curtain of the stage of life we're all from
somewhere else entirely, we are all actors on that
Shakespearian stage of life, from the universe beyond our
present seeing, where everyone is a black sheep, and all
we've done is forget it, for a while.

My life puzzle, the form of the Quest that lies
beneath life for every one of us, has been dominated by
the two forces of gender and spirituality. I used to think
they were separate issues, but now I have woken to see
that they are intertwined, like two distinct cords of one
rope, and in this singleness of being, there was the answer
to my own life puzzle.

My identity, beyond the expected, has given me the
gift of insight into gender and identity. My fascination
with the spiritual, with over forty years of meditation and
other practices, has given me further insight into my own
consciousness and how myself and my world emerges
within it. I now feel that what I used to consider to be
cursed—my ethereal nature and the gender of my heart—
is now a blessing, and I wouldn't have life any other way.
The long road back home was worth the trouble. I can

now say, with honesty, that I know who I am.

When, not so long ago, destiny gave me time on hand, and a place to work, it was time for me to write down what I'd found, the view from the edge where I look out over the countryside of my life laid out before me. I went to be alone in the wild country of North Wales, at a house I love owned by a man I love. It was clear that the only way to write about the awareness behind the mind was to write from that mind-free awareness. To do that, I put myself on the edge and stepped out into the void. I committed to write a chapter a day without knowing what I would write until I sat to write, having faith that the words would come, and every day I would know the next piece and it would appear through my fingers and make words on the screen in front of me. What an amazing five weeks that was, riding the razor's edge in breathless balance as a doorway to what lay inside me. It was a beautiful spring too, full of sunshine and unfurling leaves, a special gift in those rainy, cloudy, windy hills.

The pieces that make up this collection are simply that which emerged each day. They are not in any logical order, as if they might be going from one place to another to attain a conclusion. They appear as they appeared to me as I wrote. I see each chapter as a lens into seeing the same thing, through intellect, emotion, humour, passion; all the constituent parts of myself. The length of them all is intended to fit between stops on the bus, or stations on the train, or to fill in some time in the middle of the night when we can't sleep.

When I was going round in circles, banging my head against life at every turn, trying to find a way out of my disconnection with the world and myself, I felt like a victim of circumstance, as if a destiny that ruled me had removed my power, that I had no choice but to live as I was. But later, as I wrote in this book, I found that I was not so much a victim of circumstance as circumstance was a victim of me. Or at least my experience of life was of my own creation.

It wasn't so much that there were always choices to be made, but rather that there is always a single choice, at every turn in the road, at every unrolling of fate. We can believe in the mind and its endless, repeated stories, or we can move back into the magic of the awareness behind that mind. We can be in the small mind or the big Mind. This book is about showing that there is always an option, we can always take life another way. In this is real freedom, and in this is home for the wanderers of this world, as I used to be.

The revelation that comes with moving outside the chattering mind, even for a while, is that there is not just a sense of profound peace and belonging that comes with finding our centre. It's also the source of power, the edge, that changes not only our experience of our lives, but it changes what happens; the world is a different place. This edge comes as the secret gift of the outsider. I have found that being different, being myself, has its own power, if I can find it under the stories of powerlessness that I once told myself.

I both tell and un-tell tales, this is the essence of what I do. One form of story is useful in giving insight— like a myth or the story of an experience that tells so much—so it's good to tell, as they are a way to access the inner heart of our seeing. The other kinds of story are our own fictions, the unnoticed, unending tales we tell ourselves about who and what we are, that bind with delusion, so it's good to un-tell those, to take them to pieces and see they are made of nothing.

I begin this book with one of the stories of my own life, from more than forty years ago, when the clouds parted and I saw not through a glass darkly, but face to face, because it set the course of my life and brought me to where I am and what I write. It's the reference point for everything I write here, and it's not just my secret centre, it's common to us all.

As the irritation of the grain of sand in the oyster is that which creates the pearl, so it is that my pain with being an outsider was the source of my long and earnest search to re-find my lost self. In time, magically, the pearl appears in the oyster, as my love for myself emerged with my opened eyes, as I untold the tales of my mind and stepped into the here and now, the Pearl of Being.

2

The Boy on the Beach

One fine spring morning more than thirty years ago,
a young man, still a boy in many ways, arrived at the
jetty that was the port on the tiny Spanish island of
Formentera. He was intelligent, good looking, in fine
physical health and of an age where all things were
possible in a life that stretched out ahead of him,
apparently empty, waiting to be lived. He was also utterly
miserable, depressed to the darkest degree, almost
suicidal. Appearance and reality were distinct, as they so
often are. How talented we can be at hiding ourselves,
from ourselves and others, losing ourselves forever if we
aren't lucky, or blessed.

His troubles were not in his immediate present, not
in that jewel of a Mediterranean spring with all the hope
in the world for the taking, if he wanted it, if he knew it

was there. These troubles were in his mind, and they
eclipsed all other possibilities and realities. They had to
do with his heart-breaking sense of being an outsider who
would never belong, someone who was different, and
wrong, to himself, in being what he was in the secrecy of
his own heart. This youth on the run from himself was
burning with questions that had no answers. Who am I?
What am I? What is this life all about and why does it
hurt? Where am I going? How can I be what I don't seem
to be? His tale was full of adolescent passion and
desperation, in the days when he was making himself up
out of what he had at hand for all his life ahead. What a
powerful drama it was, none of it real in substance, but it
seemed at the time like the only reality, as our own life
dramas often do.

        He felt utterly alone, in a world where no-one
would ever understand him. He felt that the depths of his
own feelings and desires were so alien that he would
never be understood, never be accepted, that he would
always be alone in his deepest heart. These feelings were,
of course, his own feelings about himself.

        For the young man in Formentera, the agony of
those times rose to a fever pitch over a few days, when
the restless travels that had kept his black dog of dark
despair at bay came to a stop. The boats out of the island
were cancelled without reason. There now was nowhere to

go; he had to face himself, had to face his nightmares—
the lucky kid. In his loneliness and innocence of life, his
immediate experience filled with pain. The darkness of the
pain inside him overwhelmed his life. It was insufferable,
and increased over the first few days of his enforced
solitude.

Then, very early one morning, after a sweated night
of dark fears, at the end of his wits, he trudged down to
the little beach near the pension where he had taken a
simple room. The wheels of his mind were spinning out
of control. He was overwhelmed by unbearable agony,
and slumped on a washed-up log with his head in his
hands, conscious only of his screaming mind and the
emotional agony it brought to him. I can see him now in
my mind's eye, in the compassion I have for that boy in
me that is me, hunched over on that log on the golden
sand by the turquoise sea, with the warm light of dawn
warming and lighting the world all around, lost in the
hell of the dark side of a mind out of control.

The feeling of that time is in the first lines of the
poem 'The Second Coming', by William Butler Yeats:

> *Turning and turning in the widening gyre*
> *The falcon cannot hear the falconer;*
> *Things fall apart; the centre cannot hold;*

In misery, as his own circle could not hold and he

was losing all control and contact, the young man stood
and trudged back to his simple room; white walls, a bed,
a table, a chair, an ironwork image of a bull. It seemed
bleak and artificial, the light harsh, as if there was no
heart, no goodness left in this cruel world. He sat on the
edge of the bed, kicked off his sandals and turned to lie
down on the bed. His intent was to wait for breakfast, a
focus for his mind, something to do to fill in unending
time in a bleak day, a bleak life, of nothing to do, nowhere
to go, nowhere to run to. Any escape from the agony he
was in was craved for, and as he felt that he was teetering
on the edge of madness he even asked for it to take him;
perhaps there he could find some relief, anything to get
away from here. This was, to me now, the essence, the
point, the opening door. This heartfelt request was a
form of surrender; a choice was made to let go of the
attachment to the hell-creating mind into the unknown,
call it what you will as long as it is abandonment. It's the
letting go that counts.

But he was at a different kind of edge than the edge
of madness. At that very point when he could stand no
more and surrendered, let go of the grip on the agony of
mind even a little, the miracle happened. As he lowered
his head to the pillow, just a fraction above it, in that tiny
moment when attention turns to impending touch, the
spinning wheels of his mind vanished. It was as if a bubble

silently burst, and with it the skin, the division between an inner and an outer world, vanished. He was immediately in a state of electric, breathless, ecstatic peace. The room, with its chair and table and bed, was lit in a light from another world, like a vision of heaven in Renaissance art. He sat up and looked around in a new and utterly natural world without a single ripple of thought. All his dramas of misery had simply vanished like clouds before the sun. He recognised his state immediately as the *peace that passeth all understanding* he first heard of in Sunday school when he was a child. In that state of mind everything was as clear as light, effortless and brimming with an unfamiliar, but natural power.

Instinctively, he sat up, put his sandals back on and returned to the beach. What had been hell on earth just minutes before was now the Garden of Eden, the light of a Mediterranean spring reflecting off a turquoise sea, with a purple tinted island of Ibiza shimmering under a heavenly blue sky. His eyes were open; he knew he was seeing the Divine, it was simple and true. He also knew that he was that same Divine himself, that he was not distinct from the world he was seeing. His joy was inexpressible.

This classic spiritual, mystical experience gave him more than the ecstasy of the moment, the diamond crystal beauty of being—which took his heart and which was everywhere in his sight. As the day and others progressed,

he also became aware of being highly aware, acutely
conscious of every tiny detail of people, their feelings and
who they were, the tiny shifts in lines on their faces that
sent messages about the state of their being, the light of
the morning and the movement of the sea, the touch of a
breeze on his skin, the taste of sea-salt on the wind.
Everything was deep in meaning, connected and singular.

His previous confusion about who and what he was,
vanished as if it never existed. He was simply who he was,
with no questions or doubts about gender that had been
at the heart of his anguish, or family or education or work
or futures, who or what he was and where he might be
going. His adolescent clumsiness in life, bumping round in
uncertainty, tongue-tied and self-focused, also vanished.
He knew exactly what to do next and did it. Life opened
up easily before him, without effort. It hardly needed him
there at all to work in wonderful ways. Also, he belonged.
He had his divine place in this divine world, not in terms
of an assembled identity designed to please or protect,
but in terms of simply being—he simply belonged, as
rightly as the moon and the stars, the sea and the sky.

And life was easy; it flowed from one fine thing to
another. Delightful coincidences opened before him, one
after another, without effort or desire. Returning to
Barcelona a few days later the city was transformed
magically. It was as if he was seeing it for the first time, as

if the play of his life had changed from dark tragedy in a city of concrete and noise and aggression to light comedy in a fine city full of flowers and sunshine and love. Magic was everywhere, no less in his constant good humour than in the world around him. The difficult, dense, intractable world he had lived in just days before melted away. Now what he thought of tended to happen; everything that had been closed and difficult was now open and easy. He wanted nothing, he was complete without doing a thing.

In this is the secret key to everything I ever longed for; hidden within every moment, no matter how dire or mundane, there is sublime peace and profound ecstasy without reason, if only I can find it and then keep it. And the way to get to it, the way back home, has been the purpose of my life to here. The boy on the beach was and is me, of course. The tale set in Formentera all those years ago set the course for my life. Anyone who has the good fortune and Grace to have their eyes opened, as I did, has no choice but to do anything it takes to get back to being real and alive. But at least I always knew that behind the clouds there was sunshine, behind the dramas, the suffering, the apparently unending soap opera of life, there is always something luminous, crystalline and sweet. It meant that I knew there was always an option; and when there is an option there is always, no matter how deeply it may be hidden, The Choice.

3

The Woman in the Hills

I have read of people who have a revelation in
consciousness, whose minds stop and they arrive at an
open, real state of being and it is permanent; the tide
comes in and never goes out. But it went out for me. I
lost my wonderful state a couple of weeks after gaining it,
which was an almost unbearable tragedy. I remember
saying out loud, How come someone who has seen God
feels like this? Looking back with more understanding of
the way of these things, I can see that my mind was not
sufficiently trained, or purified to hold the gift of the time,
but it did give me a taste of home so I knew it existed,
and after knowing it, nothing else would ever do.

Jung talked of adolescents who had what he called
peak experiences of this magnitude then spending the
rest of their lives trying to regain what was lost, and I

recognised this as true for me. The good news is, after a long track over many years, I'm back, and now my mind is strong enough to hold what is mine. The way back home is not about the natural state, which is and always has been ours—it's handling the mind that is the task in hand, as has been said a million times over thousands of years. And it's not the mind that is the problem, not really; it's our attachment to the thoughts, stories, feelings, dramas, illusions and so on that lie between us and ourselves that is the prime issue. It took me years to get that distinction clear. It's all a question of hooks and eyes, and our interest, our fascination with our dramas, keeps us attached and dancing to the tune of the piper.

The tale of the boy on the beach demonstrates a principle that is true for us all, because although we humans are all different, at the same time we are all the same. Our dramas are incredibly diverse, but in truth a story is just a story, and what they are is nothing more than tales spun out of nothing which begin and run then fade, to be replaced by others. What is critical to understand is that we all have entrancing dramas, made in our minds, which seem real while they are being lived, and fade to nothing when the next, even more vital, drama takes to our own stage. This indicates that none of them is real, they're all just passing fantasies, every one, particularly the one we are living right now. What created misery for the boy on the beach was nothing but a mind making hell out of heaven. This is what we all do, to one degree or another, in our own particular ways and moods and colours.

This occurs not just in high dramas, but also low simple ones based on the characters we take on and believe to be what we are. Beneath it all lies the peace and wonder of our very own Self, denied us by being beguiled by the drama we believe we are living right now. It's something like having all your attention taken with a soap opera on TV, and living with all the dramas and emotions of it all—while in reality you're sitting on a fine sofa in a lovely life, which is forgotten, out of your focus while you stare at the TV and resonate with the traumas of actors on an electronic screen. One soap opera follows another, often the same one played time and time again and they come and go, but the one in front of us now is credited with the power of reality. The present is vital, alive, our most potent moment, so our present fantasies are more powerful and immediate than others. This is where we need to be sharp and note the immediacy of the present moment, and turn our attention to this speck of timeless time we are eternally riding, back within ourselves to our own unchanging awareness.

The problem is, we think it's real, this is who I am, this is my life, this story is my reality, and it's not. By believing in all this we lose what we are looking for in all the bits and pieces we collect around us to fulfil us, make us real and safe, and in the end it simply doesn't work.

What does work is being acutely aware, surrendered to reality, and in the end there is nothing else. It took me a long time, but at last I'm back to where I began on that beach, but more so. It's richer with the solidity of the years, and it's a portable feast. It hardly matters what is around me, what I possess or don't, what my name or role is in this world—it's me, the watcher, the Beingness, the consciousness itself that I am that is everything.

It's the *way* we see that matters more than *what* we see. Actually, and trickily, the way we see makes what we see. But more of that later. First of all we have to be here, and that's not as easy as it sounds. In other words, being real isn't so easy, but it's by far the best way to be, and, once you know that there is an alternative to being lost in the wondrous mind, you have The Choice.

I think of every piece in this collection that follows as pearls on a string. Writing them is offering the treasures I have gathered over the years to my friends, present and future. They are also a reminder of what I can still forget in the heat of the moment if I don't stay awake, because I still lose the best of myself at times, and I need myself to remind myself too. Truth is, since I wrote them, I keep coming back to read them once more and remind myself of what I see clearly when I am real and immediate. They really are my treasures, so there is joy in taking them out and letting them shine, like jewels, for me. Each piece is like a hologram, the same essence viewed from different ways of seeing.

At the entrance to the Pentagon, of all places, are these words from Thomas Jefferson; *The Price of Freedom is Eternal Vigilance.* This eternal vigilance is what we all need, to keep our eyes open, to stay on track, stay out of the temptation to play the game, join the soap opera and lose ourselves, again. Because if we do stay awake, it's magic, it's another world, it's freedom.

We are all tourists in this world; we arrive, lose ourselves in dramas of the day, of the life, as we do, then one day take the plane out again. A significant difference between tourists and residents is the degree of attachment to the shapes and colours and attractions around us. What we consider ourselves to be—where we think we belong— shapes the whole of our experience of life. When we have made the choice to detach from our identity and its dramas it's the same life, but sweeter and richer because we are sweeter and richer outside of the attachments of our endlessly busy minds, which create, sustain and destroy worlds for us to play out our dramas in, until we get tired of them and want to be free.

Over time I have moved from being the Boy on the Beach, seeing the world through a lens of attachment to an identity that caused misery, to the Woman in the Hills with a lens of an identity that is true to myself and that makes for me a better world. Both the boy and the woman are within me; both are me and neither are me. I can take off an identity like a mask at a carnival because it was me that made it in the first place, and behind it is me. It's the same for all of us, and I feel grateful to know this from experience.

In the end it's abandoning what we know for uncertainty, and it's an act of faith, a stepping out onto the sea of the unknown, the madness of thoughtless being, and it can be hard to let go; we do so love our suffering.

But in the end it's the single choice I have to make at every moment of my life. Am I trusting and believing that my entrancing mind is reality? Am I living the life of the outsider in my own mind, with its unending dramas and inevitable pain, or have I taken The Choice once more to be here in this pristine moment and, with this, become free of all that caused the illusion of separation, the distress of being an outsider, in the first place?

Each piece in the collection that follows is another way of looking at the same thing. It has no particular order, it doesn't follow a logical sequence of intellectual unrolling. It's just the way it came to me when I spent five weeks off in a gorgeous spring in North Wales at a house I love. Every day I wrote one piece, never planning, walking out onto the sea in faith, knowing that the only way I could write about stepping out over the edge was by doing it myself in words. Now I read it as a reminder to myself, a way to re-connect, when I have wandered into the tall tales of my inventive mind. Some spark within those words in one of the pieces I bring up, almost at random, reminds me that there is always sunshine beyond the clouds. I know again that there is always the Self a breath away, that I exist as I am and that I belong. In this knowing there is always another way of seeing, of being, is The Choice.

4
Excuse Me, Where Am I?

Our wonderful new technologies, mostly electronic wonders like this computer I'm writing on now, work in ways that are a complete mystery to me. What is the Internet, how does it work, how does it send emails at the speed of light all around the world, where does it come from? How on earth can we phone someone on a boat on the Nile, from a bus in Brighton? Come to think of it, what's electricity, how does it run down wires and light up my life? It's not the physical that is most amazing to me; it's the electronic, intangible, force behind the tangible that dazzles me most of all, and this is what lies at the foundation of everything. What we touch is nothing more than the mask of the untouchable in our touchable world.

It's no different from ourselves—like the foundations of what we are behind the bodies and roles, jobs, genders, hopes and dreams, all the things we hold in the mind that make us what we are. Is the body in the mind? Or is it the mind in the body? Best not to think about it; it can be either way round or neither, depending on what you fancy this morning, so both, or neither is true. This is how flexible the mind can be, and for that reason not to be treated so seriously, as if it was reality itself.

As for me, well, I'm still astonished by satnavs, satellite navigation systems. Turn on this little weeny thing in my hand, tell it where you want to go, and in a flash it does something miraculous, invisibly and silently, to have you nailed to within an inch on the face of the earth. Then an almost human voice begins to tell you where to go, with prescience, seeing round corners in your future, like a Guild Navigator in *Dune*. If only life was more like this, I thought, watching the dear little thing start its only act, then laughed when I realised that life *is* like this, only inside out.

How the incomprehensible satnav begins, in all its ineffable wisdom, is in finding out where you are. This much I know. Turn it on then it wakes up and next, as far as I know or guess, begins scanning the heavens to find out where you are right this moment by some kind of triangulated cleverness from satellites hovering out of sight, out of mind, above us in space. I'm innocent, haven't got a clue about how it's done and am amazed by it all. How satnavs actually do this is as incomprehensible to me as antimatter. But I do know that if the little satnav doesn't know where it is, it can't do anything, it's meaningless, just a little box without tricks.

Similarly, we too have to start with where we are, what we call *here,* if we want to go somewhere. Not too difficult for a satnav, the simple-minded little thing, it's what it was created for and it's all it can do. It's not so easy for humans in their lives, however. We have more going on; we aren't simple-minded at all, we're complex minded, and this is the problem.

All the wonder of electronic devices around us— that we love so dearly—seems to me to be based on our minds: the way we think, the way we communicate and perceive. It's all we know, it's how we work. How else could we do other than expand and empower our own facilities in miraculous ways? Anything else is outside our memories, therefore outside our imaginations. For example, instead of going to the library and looking for a book to find some information, I can flip from this programme and scan the mysterious, incomprehensible, all knowing Internet in a flash. All things that are known can be known by me in instant omniscience. The act of seeking is nothing new, it's the *way* of doing it that's different, and that's the big point. And knowing the Way with a capital W, the eternal Tao, is everything.

In the same way that I digest my dinner without knowing how I do it, or controlling it, or choosing the chemicals involved, the way I use blood, the liver, and all manner of things beyond my understanding, the Internet is travelling through my brain now, in the radio waves that connect me with fibre optic cables and high speed broadband. What is a fibre optic cable, for God's sake? How on earth are messages sent in light? But aren't I reading words right now, in light, ones that I am writing out of the imagination of my mind? What is both amazing and wonderful is that the Internet, fibre optic cables, satnavs and so on are just creations of our lovely and powerful minds. Compared to the mind we have, the consciousness we are, all of its creations are pale shadows, although they might be considered to actually *be* our minds in extension, if you like to think that way.

Some people not only understand how satnavs work, they created them. They are products of the human mind. But which mind created us? What's behind the mind that created the Internet? What's the Mind that lives in me, that lies behind the mind that creates the longings and fears and circular stories that give me some illusion of life on earth?

This is where we loop back into my beginnings in a little room on the island of Formentera—when good fortune, Grace, coincidence, the patterns of stars, destiny, readiness, compassion, surrender, and all manner of unknowns, folded time and my illusions of my own being, and let me be real, showed me what I am, and gave me a purpose for my life on earth.

This brings me to this particular moment, me: sitting on a curved brown leather sofa at the Marina in Brighton, writing and drinking coffee. The sun is shining outside the window on rows of white boats, bobbing gently in the controlled waves, costing someone a fortune. This moment is like every other moment if I am present, genuinely here and now. Before my very eyes, like a conjurer deceiving a crowd, the images in my sight, the thoughts in my mind are changing all the time. Some time ago I was at home, then I was in my car, now I am here. Later, no doubt, something else will happen. Nothing stays the same for a moment; we live in a parade of images, thoughts, sounds, smells. The trick is the detachment of the tourist, not to try to hold on to what is here or what is not, and move back into my own being, the single constant. If we think that the changes changing all around us are reality, we're lost, as we attempt the futility of grabbing and keeping them. We simply aren't fast enough, and they only exist as passing phantoms anyway.

This is the reverse satnav. Rather than reach out into the heavens to triangulate into where I am physically, or look around me for evidence of location, I turn inside and be where I am, in the place where nothing changes and from where all change is seen. Where heaven lives, what heaven is. This is the reference point for all things, the core, the fulcrum of my life.

When I get lost in my mind, when I'm tired or sick or just forgetting that the old meagre pleasures of soap opera emotions no longer suffice and I remember, what I do is to stop. I'm doing it now. I take a breath and focus back inside myself and let go. This is the point of The Choice; recognise that the game is in play and decide not to play, to see that in all the thoughts and emotions that emerge out of that moment of silence there is nothing real, it's all just dust, no matter how tempting it might be to believe they are real and so am I. In other words, I gain perspective from the point of silence, the reference point, inside my own mind. This is not just the point of relief from the eternal spinning of mind, it's also the origin of insight and best action.

It is, for me, the way to be here, the internal satnav finding me wherever I am. Here, or now, is in the space between and behind thoughts, and this is our beginning place, if we choose. If we're focused on our thoughts, believing that they're true, then dancing along to the emotions that follow them like children following the piper, we're lost.

Time to turn on the satnav, stop and watch for a crack in the forest of thoughts, contact with base and ask for the way from here. Until you're here, how can you go anywhere? And when you are here, where is there to go?

5
Einstein in the Jungle

Another of the images of our lovely, ingenious, quick minds that has come out of India, is of it being a jungle. It's as if, in so-called normal consciousness, we are lost in that jungle of the mind and can't find our way out. In the same miraculous way that our minds can imagine a jungle, they can imagine any other world on top of the one we already have. In our own imaginations of what our world is, we become trapped and lost in our own private jungle. In general we don't know this is going on; we think what we see is real, how it is, even though everyone has a different reality, which makes trillions of worlds. This makes me think that none are real, which makes me then wonder what *is* real.

Back to the boy on the beach, and the grim world of no hope and doom that was projected so skilfully upon

the paradise of a Mediterranean spring. It appeared
hopeless, so tight and dark was the jungle. But over the
dark dense jungle was light and freedom, in the same way
that sunshine shines out over the canopy of trees. By
rising higher than what gets in the way of our sight, we
will see with a simple clarity where we are and where to
go from here. The question is this; how do we rise above
the jungle of our own intricate and clever minds and see
our way out?

Well, one way of looking at it comes from the fine
mind of Albert Einstein, a favourite mythological,
archetypal genius. Hardly anyone has the slightest
understanding of his fabled $e=mc^2$ but this actually helps
in the creation of the myth. We can project our own
genius upon him more easily when there is a void of
understanding, when we are awed, when the awe within
us has someone to hang itself on so we can feel it. The
man behind the myth was highly conscious of what was
being projected upon him, and personally disassociated
himself from it, but in many ways the myth was more
powerful than the man, as they so easily can be.

One of Einstein's famed one-liners was, more or
less, this: *Problems are never solved at the level of thinking
that created them.* I say more or less because there are
variations on this quote if you look on the Internet, so in
the end we have no idea of what he actually said or wrote,

but we can choose which version fits with our own view of things. In other words, to some degree, we write our own wisdom to suit our own view of the world. I am Albert Einstein. I am awed by myself. Isn't the mind wonderful in its flexibility and ability to create credible flexible identities and other worlds?

Once more we can see how the mind spins colours over the world, in one of a million magic ways, and then we believe in our own variations as if they were the only reality, without knowing that it's what we do. That's the jungle, folks. The first step in getting out is to know that we are in it, that there is a chance that this is our own creation, and then want to get out and be free. Without knowing where we are, then having the intention to get out, we'll stay trapped and deny any problem. Or at least we'll give the source of our problems to someone or something else. God, for example. Or the Devil. Or my wife, my mother, my boss, any of the characters in the drama of my life. Anything, anybody but me.

As we spend much of our lives trying to solve the problems we live with, this Einstein comment has been pored over for many years by many. Mostly, I guess, creating more and more ideas at the same level of thinking, because the level of thinking from which we look at it does not have the capacity to lose itself and go higher. Round and round we go in our dog-chasing-tail lives. At least that was my proud way of doing things, the way I was taught, following the traditional patterns of working harder at what doesn't work when it fails me again, my tail an inch from my jaws. I know, I'll run faster, make more effort, more money, more power, take another wife or husband, this will make my life work, make me feel complete, perhaps, for a while.

I prefer to consider levels of consciousness rather than levels of thinking, as the way we think actually comes from our level of consciousness, which also rules our perception and our feelings. We all experience different levels of consciousness, or states of mind, on a daily, hourly, second by second basis, but most of the time don't notice what is happening. Some people still think the world out there is real, an amazing belief in this day and age, when everyone has their own world to believe in, one which changes in detail and feeling all the time. One morning I'm just fine, happy, grateful for life on earth, I like my body, my friends, my life, I'm optimistic and cheerful. The next day I wake up on the wrong side of the bed, grumpy and miserable, can't stand my friends, my lover, my life; I'm pessimistic and dark. The world looks like a different place from either state, our feelings about it are different, our predictions of the future are different, but it's the same world, and we are the same people.

What has changed is our outlook, the place we are seeing it from, which changes not only how we see it but what we see. One of the very best ways of measuring my state of mind is with my closest Friend. If she seems impossible, difficult, moody and unreasonable, I've got problems—not with her, but with me. Other days, and other times, and she will seem like a Goddess full of wisdom and good cheer. I can see where I am in myself by how she seems. The more contracted my state, the less I am willing to let go of my attachment to her clearly-visible shortcomings—yet another measure of my state. Round and round we go, the more contracted we are, and the harder we try, the faster we run to nowhere. Why am I so tired all the time?

The varieties of levels of consciousness, states of mind, are infinite. Think of a scale from suicidal depression to godlike ecstasy, as with the boy on the beach, and a dazzling range of intricate, shifting possibilities in between the two extremes. In any one day we vary as our moods rise and fall, as our state of mind expands and contracts. The trick is not to get too involved, not to get into the drama as your own, not to take the eternally shifting world personally. Then you are not the mood, the state of mind, rather you are that which experiences it. It takes practice, it takes wanting to be free, it takes time, but it's worth it.

In essence, watching and being detached from the shifting tides of levels of consciousness is no different from being the same person at 15, 25 and 50. We are the same watcher, unchanged. Our experience is different, however, according to how we have learned to see. If we can practise focusing on that which sees, the part of us that doesn't change, then the credibility of the passing state diminishes, and we are more free. This in itself makes for an expansion of state, but it takes really wanting to, persistence, and eternal vigilance, to become free.

For sure, the higher we go, the more expanded we go, the more we can see. Just as being lost in the jungle is solved by climbing the highest tree and thereby seeing the entire wood, its end, the river beyond and the way to get home, so it is true that expanding our own mind gives us the ability to see not only where we are, but the way to go from here. Doing it is The Choice.

6

The Snakes in the Mind

One great old way of getting in touch with the deeper part of ourselves, where our treasures lie, is in the telling and listening to stories, myths, poems and songs. In some magic way they can lead us down past the rule of the mind and all its obsessions, to the simplicity and naturalness of our truth.

There is a wonderful story that comes from India, the subcontinent that looks on a map like the heart of the world. As in all spiritual traditions stories, or parables, are told to give a sharp insight into some essential truth, in a sweet form that is palatable for little children or what little children grow up to be. And, like all classic tales that resound with some essence of what it is to be human, they can be told over and over again, getting better with time. The simplicity of these tales can be deceptive—

some I have heard time and time again over the years,
thinking that I understood them as far as they go, and
then another onion skin layer is peeled away with the
passing of time and changes wrought in me, to reveal yet
another teaching that goes to the essence of what we are.

The story of the rope and the snake is one of those
tales that has spread around the world, and because
many of us know it so well, it is even easier to let it take
us into ourselves and see it from another angle, from
another place, because it's all about seeing, the sight
from within, insight.

ॐ

Two men are walking along a road in twilight. Lights are
coming on in the villages all around, and the quiet of the
evening is all around them. Then, as they turn a bend in
the road they see something shadowy lying all looped in
coils across the track ahead of them. They panic, fill with
instant fear, and start shouting. 'Snake! Snake on the
track!'

They are so frightened that they hold back, they
know not to come too near to snakes, so they wait till a
group of men from the nearby village come running with
lanterns, further sticks in hand to beat the snake to death.

Although the snake still hasn't moved, by the time
the lights arrive there is group of people, attracted by the

excitement, yabbering on in fear in the shadows, telling stories of past snakes and the misfortunes that follow them, stories of terror and pain and death. Fear and excitement fill the air as all the horrors of snakes in the night are brought up and let live in the fertile imaginations of all the people, practised—as are we all—in the art of the inner creation of drama. This is one of the things our minds do well all by themselves. They have no need for us to interfere and guide them into the creation of horror stories, they're on automatic and do it all by themselves.

Then the men with the lanterns arrive, and cautiously approach the snake, which still hasn't moved a muscle. Closer and closer they creep, hardly breathing, sticks held high to finish the snake off once and for all before it poisons all their children, bites their wives and brings unwelcome death.

Then one of them laughs, reaches forward and takes hold of the snake and waves it in the air. 'Look,' he cries, holding it up high, 'it's not a snake, it's a rope!'

Of course, the men who first saw the rope in the half light, and the onlookers who came to join in the game start to laugh too. Fear is transmuted in an instant into laughter and relief. What was seen as danger through false perception is nothing at all when light is brought to bear. Illusion of danger creates real fear as much as true danger. Unreality is as powerful as reality in the creation of how we think and feel.

It's about illusions that make us believe things that may or may not be true, how our dubious perceptions and limited understandings create our realities. Each one us lives in a different world, according to how we perceive it, and that can change moment by moment, hour by hour, day by day. Billions of different worlds in this world, all apparently real, each the foundation of a life. Where's reality in all this? See a snake, then your reality is a snake and fear is yours, no matter if it is a rope.

Imagine a life without belonging, being a stranger forever; unacceptable, tainted, simply not good enough, and that will become your reality. As will the pain that follows. It's the story of the boy on the beach; young and intelligent and healthy, with a mind full of misery. Which tale is more real, the boy or the snake? Which tale do we believe? The answer is none of them. They're all as tangible as dreams, and like dreams they come and go like the wind.

The key to the art of life is being aware, learning how to see. If we just hear the story of the rope and the snake again without being aware of what's going on in it, what it means about how we live our lives, what is actually real—what's the point? We'll find it amusing then we'll move on to the next movie, the next episode in our soap opera, written, directed and acted in by ourselves, and live in a snake-pit, because that is what we perceive.

The men walking in the evening don't look properly, so they don't see what they are looking at. With just the simplest of visual clues they react, they respond to what they perceive as being a snake, which only exists in their minds. The snake does exist, but *in* there, not *out* there. Notice that they don't see something benign; they are looking for the trigger of fear, not something to love, because they have become addicted to the rush of fear, the emotions of tragedy. Day after day our TVs and movie screens are filled with stories of tragedies, misery, pain and death, because of that addiction to the dark side of feelings. Addictions are hard to break; we love them too much.

This is how we are, we humans, forever creating fear, like the boy on the beach who never was me, really, at the depths of reality. Our lovely minds, a divine creation that can make a wonderful world—and does, if let off the leash—will create hell, or snakes. It's those minds of ours that colour the world we live in, without our consent, without our being conscious of what we are doing, so we blame something or someone else for our suffering.

Then the people who come to see what the fuss is all about immediately fall in with the created fear, and talk amongst themselves to whip up the collective feeling, so to enhance the original misperception and its children, the dark fears, and yet another temporary reality springs into being. Welcome to newspapers and the TV news, friends gossiping over coffee, the world of the collective thought, collective unreality that has created strife, misery and wars from the beginning of time.

What makes the difference is light: when the men with lanterns come, so they can see what is really on the path. The instant they can see, there is recognition of reality, and fear turns into joy and laughter. It can happen in an instant, and in this way we are immediately free of all our undeserved fear.

So it's all about our minds, our perceptions, our fears, our projections of snakes in our minds onto an innocent world, and then becoming aware of reality and becoming free. The question is; how do we attain this?

It's all in the story. First of all we have to want to see. Intention is at the source of action. If you see that you make up stories that mask reality and cause fear, even that there might be a possibility that this happens sometimes, then you might want to see, so you can be free of it. This is the beginning that counts, The Choice to see clearly. In time it turns darkness into light in the simplest of ways so then we can see what's going on around us, and more often than not what was seen to be a snake turns into a rope. What this means for us all is that we can see the source of pain and fear in our lives is in the mind, as it so often is, and when this is clear, instead of living a tragedy full of fear and unhappiness, we too can laugh at the comedy.

7
How Not to Be
What You Aren't

Words are not the best of means to show us any other way than the one that got us here. These little gods and demons that are right this moment popping up on the page in front of me are deeply alluring, creative, so powerful that they create our worlds, often without us understanding how they work, where their power comes from, quite what they are doing to us. Dictators rise to power on words—ideas made concrete—teenage girls are bullied to death with poisonous words, a woman marries a man with two words and opens a door to a dynasty, ideas turned into words create giant business corporations, revolutions, ecstasy and misery, salvation and early death.

We create our ideas of what we are with the force inherent in words. I am a man, I am a woman, I am French, I am a soldier, I am an accountant, I am gay. Each of these statements of identity has wide consequences that ripple out from the simple statement to every corner of our lives. They shape not only who we think we are, they shape our responses, opinions, the way we walk, the way we think, the way the world looks to us, what we consider reality to be. Our opinions come from our assumed identities, from the bundle of memories that make us into what we think we are, as far as we are attached to these ideas, these mentally-held images.

Words exist in the world of opposites, where most of us live. There is no woman without man, there is no black without white, up and down, in and out, bent and straight, feeble and strong, young and old, on it goes. When we get all tied up in our words, the expression of our ideas and feelings, we can't see beyond them. In fact we think there is nothing beyond our words, there is nothing but the jungle, that this is where the answers are. Round and round we go, stumbling in circles through the jungle of our minds.

I was working recently with a group of senior officers in the police, which is organised within a strict hierarchy, with clear ranks and badges; it is based on a military model and is masculine in structure and viewpoint. About one in ten of these interesting and powerful people were women. I am always fascinated by issues of power, perception and gender, because they are matters that have affected my life so deeply, so these women were fascinating to me, as they seemed to break some essential rule. I was intrigued by a woman who was feminine, light, and at the same time not someone to be taken lightly. She wielded significant power over many men. I asked her if she was ever hassled, ever had trouble, was ever put down because she was a feminine woman in this male world. Never, she said cheerfully, not once. Fascinated, I asked why. She thought for a moment then said, with great simplicity and effect: 'It's because I know who I am.'

This didn't mean that she knew she was a woman, or a police officer, or British, or any of the other social identities we normally consider to be what we are. It was a statement that transcended all of those and went to the core of what or who she was. This kind of simple self-knowledge has a resonance that all of us feel, as every one of us is acutely conscious of where people are in themselves; what we relate to as ourselves shines out as a message to the world. Generally, we are not aware of this foundation of relationship, the subtle messages that shape how we interact with people, as forces that help shape our worlds.

Once I was talking to a friend about being 'hit on', being approached for relationship, and I wondered why this never ever happened to me, even though I know, or imagine, I am attractive to some. My friend laughed, and said, 'You've got a big sign on your forehead saying: Not available, Keep away; that's why you're never approached.'

Now this was not true in the literal sense, but when I considered what she said, I realised that it was true in the subtle way of a projection of feeling, a kind of coloured force-field that surrounds me, and which people read so clearly that it shapes my relationships, helps make my world. All of us do this, of course, both as creators and receivers. Why are some people picked on, others not? How come some people stand out as capable, even when they aren't? Why is it that we come to some people for tenderness or another form of love and know we are safe? Why do some people make us feel afraid just by walking into the room?

Once more, the physical world we live in is formed from the subtle, the intangible. We begin with the deepest and faintest of feelings, longings, aversions, these then form into conscious thoughts, which may then move on into words, spoken or written. This is what is going on now with me, my subconscious triggering the conscious which then moves into my fingers as I write. The words on the page are the physical markers of what exists within me, almost like doors that open and let out the real force that lies beneath my waterline. Writing like this is a revelation of what is inside me, of who I am; as you read the words you can see through them like little lenses into what is going on in me. Or, put another way, these words are a means for me to project myself out into the world, into whoever reads them.

We don't need to state what we think about ourselves for it to be seen, read, and reacted to. More business is done at the invisible level than the visible, but it isn't just the conscious that is affected by the subconscious, it works backwards too. This means that we can choose our thoughts, as well as the feelings that go along with them and give them juice, flavour, real power, and this then works back into the core feelings and messages we give to the world, which make us who we are.

It's our attitudes that we can shift and mould with awareness, in the same way that I brought the attitude of gratitude to my father on his deathbed, and the complex resonances of that choice changed my experience of life. That life-changing experience was created out of words which were powerful gateways to feelings. As always, we need to be aware, to know that there is The Choice. More often than not we unconsciously identify the bundle of attitudes that govern our created worlds as being how it is, simple reality; but if we can take a step back and see that these attitudes and their offspring, our thoughts and words, are not who we are but what we possess, what we do, we also have the choice to change, and create a sweeter world to be sweeter in.

This act of awareness, becoming conscious of our minds, feelings, attitudes, convictions, brings us back into ourselves. If I am not all these things, what am I? It's no different from the police officer who knew who she was, so she was out of reach from hassle for being what may be perceived as a woman with power in a masculine world.

It was clear to me that she didn't for a moment believe in the story of being a woman, the collection of ideas, beliefs, fears, outrages and feelings and that might have made her into less than she was. Believe in that story, and this is what you will project, give out to the world as reality, then your world will form within the shapes of your attitudes and bingo, there's your reality.

It might be useful to create a better story to shift things into a more comfortable shape, but best of all is to eradicate the words that make the tale in the first place. What is there left? Just you. When we take the step into this Being-ness without a story, the old stories are freaked out. What will you be, who will you be, without a tale to tell yourself?

Just me, naked and simple. And when we come from this place of just me, simply being, the world takes on a different shape. It's the usual case of subtraction as another way of moving on; we don't need to add more to the ideas of what we think we are to make sense of the game, we need to take away things, in the end everything, until there really is nothing left but everything.

In all the flurry of words in the mind or in the mouth, it can seem impossible to find a way out, to find a just world that recognises me for who I am. But we always have to begin with ourselves. First just be here and now, where we always are as the creator or watcher of the words, and we will see that we aren't them at all, we are what stands behind them. This is the act of recognition that begins to change our worlds; this is the conscious choice. If we know who we are at this level of being, people can tell, they really can, and so can we. Without the old filters, the words and stories that we believed made us safe, our lives shift and open, and we become who we are, not who we aren't. Knowing myself like this is the sweetest feeling I know.

8

Thanks, Dad

We who are like senseless children shrink from suffering,
but love its causes. We hurt ourselves; our pain is self-
inflicted! Why should others be the object of our anger?

Shantideva

I am writing these words in my home from home, one home of my heart, in Peter's house up in the hills of North Wales. I love it here, with all its wind and rain and wildness and extravagant beauty. This part of Wales is where I used to come as a child. I stayed at Colomendy, which was the place that kids from Liverpool used to come to for a taste of the wilder part of the world. It's lovely to be back, fifty years later. Outside the window, part of the house, is the garden I designed and put together over ten years ago, with its huge heart-shaped pool, 100 tons of

great rocks, the stone circle assembled with ancient
geometry and the shrine to the Goddess made from
telegraph poles, and a triple spiral of the three aspects of
the Goddess made from roofing tiles over slate. I love it.

I was here with Janie in a warm and summery
September when the call that will always one day come
came from my sister in law. 'If you want to see your father
alive,' she told me, 'you'd better come now.' My feelings
were mixed; he was my one and only father, and at the
same time I had decided I never wanted to see him again.
I believed in a story I told myself at that time, that he had
been nasty to me and had hurt me, and I could never
forgive him. I was a victim of cruel fate. And so on. It's a
familiar tale in our world, so deep it belongs in the
collective consciousness that it is almost encouraged to
emerge and take form. It's easy to find other people to
sympathise with that one. Me too! They say, me too, and
look, we share yet another created world.

But what could I do? I simply had to go, and made
ready to leave to drive down to the hospital in Swindon,
where he was dying. I was about to drive off when Janie
tapped at the window. I lowered it and she said; 'You
need to thank him.'

'Thank him?' I said, uncomprehending. 'Thank
him?'

She nodded. 'Yes, thank him.'

I drove off, and for the next four hours as I drove south I kept repeating to myself, Thank him? Thank him? For what? How could I thank someone who had reduced me to tears so many times? What would happen if he turned on me again, reviled me once more? What would happen if he scorned me again? Could I fight with a dying man? Thank him? How could I thank him? I kept repeating, trying to find a place for this mad idea in the story I had created of my life, and failing.

Thank God for our friends, for the love of friends— something new had been inserted into the almost rigid tale of my life, and I was placed in the fertile ground of uncertainty, where there is hope for change and the unfolding of love.

That same afternoon I sat at his bedside with my mother. I was so profoundly shocked at the way the cancer was destroying him that my heart filled with compassion. Things had changed; the ground I stood on had shifted in this place of profound sickness and impending death. My mother left first and I drew close to him, looking directly into his eyes, took his hands in mine and said:

'I want to thank you.'

'Thank me?' he asked. 'But I haven't been a good father for you.'

'You gave me life,' I said, 'looked after me, brought me up, you gave me so much.' As I said it, I felt it—this

was a deeper reality than the passing anguish, the dramas
of hurt, rejection and misunderstanding, of the last few
years. In that close silence we shifted from trivial
mindstuff to the reality below it, and met in a different
place than we known for many years. We came to the
love that lay beneath the storms of life, our single heart.

He paused, looking deeply into me for some time.
'Are we all right now?' he asked, perhaps the most critical
question of my life.

'Yes,' I replied as my heart soared open. 'We're all
right now.'

I hugged him and left. That was the last time I saw
my father. He died the next day. There are no loose
threads, not a trace of the unfulfilled with my lovely
father, who gave me life and love. As for what I once
perceived as unforgiveable, well, there is nothing to
forgive.

Part of the story I was telling myself at that time
was that the relationship with my father would never be
resolved this life, that the wounds ran too deep. It was a
good storyline that fitted in with my then current models
of despair, founded on some deeply satisfying sense of
being wronged, powerless yet good at heart. It would fit
well with the mood of the times, the psychologically
semi-informed way of thinking that had created its own
myths, based on my needing to be fixed, because I was

broken. In truth, all that needed fixing was the way I thought, the story I had made up and that had shaped my view of the world, who I thought I was, how I had acted. It's our responses, the nature of how we respond to something that happens, that shapes our futures, and I could understand my previous responses to my father by the experience of life I used to live.

What was behind my story was an attitude, a way of seeing. I had developed a certain conviction about what was true, about my father and about me, and our roles in the play were set. Mixed up with the attitude and the belief was a fine undercurrent of feeling that gave the whole drama its fire and life. All of this complexity existed at a certain state of mind, a contraction of consciousness, which in itself supported the thoughts, the feelings and everything that happened.

Perhaps the most significant aspect of the attitude that created an apparent reality was resentment, rage, towards my dear old dad. He wasn't being what he should have been. He should have accepted my radical shift of identity as easily as having a cup of tea, even though I found my change of essential persona almost impossible to deal with myself. Where did the feelings begin? Who really found me difficult to take? In the end, is there really anything out there at all?

When Janie told me to thank him, she was invoking

an ancient power. An embedded attitude of anger at
someone, or something, can be transformed with the
power of gratitude. So deep does our love of our rage lie,
we feast on the feelings of righteous anger and are
unwilling to let go. It's all someone else's fault anyway,
we are powerless to change. Even if we could, it wouldn't
make sense, because we can see the abuse in the guilty
one.

But on that afternoon, circumstances had changed.
My father was on the brink of his own death, and he knew
it, as I did. I instinctively knew the importance, to him and
to me, of reaching out to him, with love. For both of us,
the time for pride had gone. I made the magic choice; I
thanked him, he accepted the thanks, a form of gratitude
unto itself, and the whole game was turned upside down
in a moment.

Did he need to be on the point of death to be open
enough to ask if we were all right now, having accepted
gratitude? Did he need to be on the point of death for me
to offer gratitude? We could have done this years ago,
but for our pride, our love of the story we had written,
the drama we adored, the feelings we encouraged. Either
one of us could have chosen a difference in the game we
played, if we had been willing to let go, as I did, with a
little judicious prompting.

We can make the choice to practise the gift of

gratitude any time, with any situation, the more that
there seems to be nothing to be grateful for, the better.
As with myself and my father, the willingness to show
gratitude can change our world. We can be grateful for
the air we breathe, the bodies we have, no matter how
they are. We can feel gratitude for our families, our planet,
our friends, our enemies, rain on a picnic. In just the same
way that new clothes can feel a little odd at first, until we
get used to them, so it might feel odd to be grateful, until
we get used to it, but it's worth persevering.

   The price is the loss of rage, anger at the world, all
those juicy dark feelings that we adore, that we are
addicted to. At first it's tough, it feels wrong, as if there is
a space that needs to be filled. Without my dramas, what
am I? When I began to drop mine and be in the void of
unattachment to my sorry tales, which was full of light
and happiness, my mind whispered that I would be bored.
Turn the TV on, we can't stand the silence, I can't abide
being so close to myself. It was like missing the next
episode of my favourite soap—The Trials and Tribulations
of Persia West—missing all the dark feelings of loss,
betrayal, grief and so on.

   But with practice the new attitude becomes real,
and then something in the world out there, for example a
father, will change on the spot. It takes no time at all to
get used to being happy, in ecstasy even, as we undo the

hooks and eyes of our attachments to the ten thousand things that make us what we aren't.

This showed me that my attitudes, my feelings, which I mistook for realities, are as flexible and changeable as the wind, and are subject to my own will. It's me that made that world of strife and unforgiveness, blame, separation, and when I decided that I'd had enough, I shifted my realities to find that none of the darkness existed outside of me at all.

This is The Choice as the essence of freedom. Any one of us at any time can choose to see anyone or anything in our world as worthy of our gratitude. It's nothing other than a form of love; as I thanked my father, the doors of the heart opened, and as I changed myself, my world changed too—it became heaven on earth.

As William Blake wrote: *Gratitude is Heaven itself.*

9
Spiders on the Bus

A while ago I was travelling into town on the bus, in my favourite place at the front on the top of the double-decker where I can see everything, even pretend I'm driving, if I'm alone. The seat next to me was taken by a man and a woman who followed me up the stairs. While I basked in the early spring sunshine and relished the joy of the first blossoms and a glimpse of the sea shining in ecstasy in the distance, they began to talk.

'Miserable bugger', said the man. 'Bus drivers never used to be so unfriendly.'

'God, yeh, bloody miserable, that's the word, miserable,' said the woman. 'You see the expression on his face?'

'Sour, didn't give a damn about us. He could've smiled or something.'

'Why don't they train them properly?' the woman
demanded. 'They weren't like this when we were kids,
they used to be a cheerful bunch.'

'You're right. The world isn't what it used to be.
Nowadays ....'

And so on. And on. The minute we hear the
fearsome word 'nowadays' we know this means that there
will now be a comparison with a better golden world that
doesn't exist and never did, and only exists as a measure
for all the failings we perceive in the present. Those
golden days of a sunlit childhood when the world had
better values, people loved each other, cared for each
other in neighbourly ways, when men married women
and they were always happy, when bus drivers were
cheerful as they whistled their way along the golden road
to happytown. It's cuckoo land, and exists only in the
minds of the desperate, or lost.

These kinds of fault-finding patterns of words are
always untrue, always tiresome, always destructive of the
time we are living, and the truth is that there is no other.
When was it ever not now? The only time we are ever in
is now, the only place is here. Outside the window of the
bus, bouncing down the road to paradise *in* paradise,
there was the divine glory of spring, the revelation of the
Goddess dressed in the ultra-green, viridissima, and
sunshine, pulsing with hope and light and new

beginnings. Joy, and the silent unfolding of a billion folded
leaves, resonated with the same divine nature inside
myself.

Next to me, deep in dark fantasy, two people were
sharing the view of a world created in their own minds by
words and feelings, shared in dark passion. While the real
world blazed in glory and I, in my good fortune, blazed
with it, all they could see was their unhappiness. The more
they talked, the more I could see how they were creating
a world of their own. Not only were they busy knitting a
view of life out of yarn they had used many times before; I
could see that they had no idea of what they were doing.
They thought they were seeing reality, and described
what they saw, then relished the emotions those words
created. In fact, for them, it *was* reality, made in agreed
gloomy colours chosen unconsciously from the dark
paintbox of their own minds.

They were not, of course, describing the bus driver,
the innocent guy who gave them tickets without bursting
into song or greeting them like Emissaries of the Emperor
of the Universe as they bought single bus tickets to the
station. What they were describing was themselves. They
were telling me of their attitudes, what they believed and
how they felt about it all, how they felt about their lives,
how unhappy they were, the poor loves. The sour face
was their own, the unwelcome was their own, the flawed

world was their own.

Then, not wanting to recognise themselves in the dark shapes of words and feelings that lay within their minds and hearts that hurt them so much, they projected them onto the innocent bus driver, who was neither friendly nor unfriendly. His sin, and the opportunity it gave, was that he was expressionless as he took our money then drove his great big bus off down the road. What a wonderful world it is, where buses come along the road near my home, tracked 'nowadays' by satellite systems that can tell me on this very computer how many minutes I have to wait for the next number 27. Not only that, they have people who play the part of drivers in our cosmic drama, to make it possible that I can travel into town, day and night no matter what the weather. Praise the Lord!

So, within a wonderful world, another, not so wonderful, is created. As I listened to my teachers on the bus, I vowed yet again not to fall into this trap once more. Be present, I thought, make the choice so you don't get ensnared by the fantasies of your mind running round unsupervised, like a spoiled terrier or toddler doing what it likes as it seeks boundaries, which are recognised by the presence of pain. If I indulge my mind by losing myself in one of its dramas, then I live in a different world in this world. What I lose is the greater world, one of simple presence, being here now, where it is eternally spring. My travelling companions were reminding me of how I too had created one dark world after another for myself in my own life, and how sometimes, when I am tired or ill, the inclination to wander into my own version of a darker world still exists, in seed form, to be recognised and caught before it wreaks havoc in my life—I hope. Unless I was willing to always drop the game and be aware, turn off the inner TV and all its soap operas, I'd still be in it, lost again. Once an addict, always an addict, the choice is not to indulge and spiral down into unhappiness. Not just that; I'd also lose the divine power of Being that throbs in me without end, free and without even a satellite dish, creating a fresh and wonderful life all on its own, in shapes out of light and joy, if am its constant servant.

The people on the bus, who were creating their own universes, gods to themselves, had lost touch with greater reality, if they had ever known it in the first place. There they were in a perfect spring in perfect view, and they were working hard at removing it all from sight and mind. We are like spiders, the Guru said, spinning webs in a corner of a room. The room is God's creation, God in fact, the universe as it is, the shining spring in every moment. The web is our own creation, a lesser world within the world that we make in our own minds, and which entrances us. Like spiders focused entirely on the creation of their webs, we focus entirely on the creation of our own minds, and as all we see is our own web, that's all there is, there is no choice, we live in a world of miserable bus drivers, miserable everyone, miserable ourselves.

Awareness is the key, the provider of the choice, since unawareness of how we work, and attachment to our unending tales, deny it. If I am aware that what I assume to be reality is nothing more than a web I am spinning on the 27 bus, or a on a beach in Spain, or in an argument at work, then I have the choice to unhook from the fantasy— if I prefer freedom. Nowadays I keep on checking. Am I here and now, making the single eternal choice? Am I in my mind, dancing to the ancient rhythms of my own thoughts as they travel round and round, telling me the same worn out tales? Or am I free? It's easy to tell, once you've seen a rat, you know all rats.

Frankly, I'm bored by the stories I used to believe in, so faithfully. Do I have no imagination at all, so I have to repeat the same tales, day in, day out? Is it time to write another story altogether, or, and here's radical freedom— not have a story at all? Maybe it's best if I keep well out of the way, and just let that thoughtless intelligence behind my intelligence create my life from this point onwards. How relaxing, how amusing it is when I do, how warm and safe and full of love; why would I ever want to lose this?

And maybe I should not beseech God to provide for me in the way I think best. Saint Theresa of Avila once said that more tears were shed over prayers that were answered than over those that were not, so maybe it's better not to pray for what we think we want. That's just the same game all over again. Where's the cosmic surrender when we go that way? Doesn't the Self, the divine essence of ourselves that created infinite galaxies and whiskers on kittens have no imagination to suit me, yet another of its creations, better than by repeating the limited repetitions of my mind?

It's the story of the beach in Formentera all over again in another disguise at another time with other actors, but the principle is just the same. Within each moment of time, no matter how we might feel, there is another way of seeing, there is another way of Being. We spiders have the choice to tear apart our webs and light up the world in any instant.

10

No Wildlife in
this Forest

Imagine a city kid like me going off into the forest to see
the wonderful creatures that live there. While I reckon
I'm being pretty stealthy, to the animals that live there
I'm stomping and clumping round like a storm on legs,
twigs breaking, leaves crackling, announcing my alien
presence magnificently and they all know I'm there, for
miles around. So, wisely, they are deep in their burrows,
high in their nests, invisible to me. 'No wildlife in this
forest,' I think to myself, while a thousand bright eyes
watch me pass.

In something of the same way, the intelligence of
women is often unseen by men, or perhaps more precisely,
the feminine is not valued or recognised by the masculine.

This is true of the masculine in women as much as the feminine in men, so it's not a simple game of women and men, as clearly and badly delineated as skirts and trousers on toilet doors. Having walked some fascinating tracks between the genders, which actually led me to the place of not believing they actually exist, I've been granted a perspective that sees beyond the obvious. Essentially, if we aren't what we think we are—which we aren't—genders, which exist only in thought and vary across time and space, definitely aren't what we are.

I clearly saw the power relationship between so-called women and men when I was working with a group of women recently. We were talking openly, with great insight, about the affairs of the organisation they belonged to. Then a man approached the group. He was of middle rank in the organisation, not someone who demanded immediate attention due to rank. But still, the air changed instantly. On the spot the conversation stopped and attention was placed on the guy. It was as if the TV had changed channels. Many of the women smiled. This is often a way of showing compliance, a statement of recognition of rank, it's a way of pleasing, relating by being pleasant to look at and thereby often being lost from view. The women didn't tell him that something important was going on, please let us get on with it, but turned their attention to his needs, even though doing so broke up the flow of what we were doing. The thread was lost.

Now in this—unremarked but known—is that the man, even though he was not a leader in the hierarchy, simply expected, in all his simple humility (he was a nice guy) to take the attention of the group, and was given it. This shows much about the game we play. Note that it is played by both genders, as in it taking two to tango.

We don't consciously do this; on the whole, we don't decide that these are the roles we play. It's as if this is the given role, it has been assigned and it just happens and here we are. Even though I was acutely conscious of what was going on when the man came and interrupted our discussion, I actually found myself smiling, showing my teeth too, acting the part that came with the identity I had taken on as the recognisable evidence of who I am. How would people relate to me otherwise? If the image is not clear, people get worried, uncertain, don't know what to do, don't know who they are relating to. Even though I was conscious of doing it, the force of circumstance and the collective role overwhelmed me, and I did what was expected. Then I got annoyed; with myself, with the way life is, bloody men, bloody women, and with that fell into the automatic responses that are almost traditional for women.

The most important point here is this teaching I

learned in India, a core teaching that keeps on unfolding over time: your responses create your destiny. Best to be conscious of our responses, particularly if they are invisible, which means we need to learn to see them, we need to become aware so we can become more free.

The point here is that there was no way our male visitor could have been conscious of the intelligence of the group of women whose conversation he had impinged upon. The unconscious roles and the responses they brought denied reality. Not so different from the absent little forest creatures, the wisdom and intelligence of the women was unseen, unrecognised, so it might never have existed. When this goes on without us being aware of it, what it means is that we see only a part of the world we live in. Our sight is blinkered. This isn't about women and men so much as how we see or, more importantly, how we don't.

The reason these games go on is that we adopt our roles unconsciously, and then unconsciously play the games that come with the roles, either as man or as woman or anything else: police officer, shop assistant, prostitute, President. Even though the games we play may not suit who and what we are, collective expectation can be far stronger than our own identity. And it does take two to tango; there is no woman's role without a man's, no man's without a woman's. Both of these genders, and the forces that live beneath them, yearn for balance, integrity, both in our outer lives and our inner lives.

Of all the aspects or qualities of our lives, the female and male, man and woman, yin and yang, are fundamental. As with all things, what we see on the outside is a clear reflection of what is inside. So when one aspect of our inner world is out of balance, for example in one side being dominant, seen, recognised, valued, resented, or denied more than another, there is an imbalance in our outer world.

The forest, the wildlife, the rivers, the oceans are the ground from which we exist, the sands upon which the horses race. Going deeper into ourselves, the same principle can be seen in our consciousness. There are thoughts, desires, identities, plans and so on, but they exist only because of the foundation of pure consciousness on which they play. The thoughts, the movements of the mind, are more tangible, visible and credible, but if we only take note of this part of our existence another part is denied by being invisible. The two are intertwined, are the two faces of the single genderless unity that is the divine, that is our essence. Within each of us is a mixture of these essential forces, and the particular blend that is our own nature is a foundation of the delight of what we are.

The way to get to see the elusive forest creatures is to be still and quiet and wait and watch, in essence to

become part of the forest itself. It's an act of surrender;
now I will obey the ways of the forest. The way to get to
recognise the elusive power of the feminine, either
within or without, is to be aware, to step outside of the
usual game of belief in the creations of the mind, and be
alert. Then we can see the wildlife, by becoming still, by
blending into the context, by being part of nature. On
the whole it's easier for women than for men, of course,
because they are often there already. They don't have to
go in search of the feminine foundation of the universe,
they are it already.

It's easier to see masculine power than feminine
power—it's more evident when value is on the
masculine—but if we only recognise, value, believe in
one aspect of what we are, we're out of balance, and
there's no wildlife in this forest.

Having created one gender identity to please the
world around me—look, I'm normal!—and then dissolved
it to create another in its place, I know the whole thing is
fantasy, not just for me but for us all. I've come to love
the shifting balances of the being that I am, the mixture
of feminine and masculine that is me, because now I
have come to letting them form their own balance, I am
balanced, I know who I am behind the roles, projections
and fantasies that came with a rigid sense of gender.

People talk of this in terms of being and doing, the

active and the passive, the masculine and the feminine, and they are all right, because the world is as we see it. If we can move to the balance point behind all of this, rather than focus on one or the other, or even both, then something miraculous happens. My existence in this world is due to the meeting in balance of the masculine and the feminine, in the form of my mum and dad. How astonishing it is; what immeasurable power lies in this fusing of equal forces.

How might this work, how does this work, in our lives and within our own beings? What power might our own inner and outer fusion bring? Maybe it's time to take a chance and find out, step over the edge of our limitations into the great void, let the yin and yang balance beautifully of their own accord and let them create the children of our own beings, in whatever shape, form, quality, essence of masculine and feminine that they may be at heart.

Then the silent forest erupts with wildlife, not a feather of which is controlled by us, not a whisker of which we could equal in ingenuity and microscopic perfection, and we can know that what we see out there is nothing other than the wonder of myself.

11

Garden of My Heart

In the early nineties I went back to school. I needed a new
job, what I had been doing no longer worked, I was in a
blind alley of life. So I followed some wise guidance, and
went off to learn gardening. This was such a radical vector
from the track of life I'd been following that I felt deeply
nervous, a fine and good sign. It meant I was moving out
of familiar tracks, the comfortable ruts that were being
trodden deeper and deeper with passing time, but which
I was familiar with, so had unconsciously chosen over the
unknown quantity of inspired freedom. I would never
have moved out of the painful familiar without love and
wisdom from outside myself, as my imagination was
limited by the past and my scared mind would only
repeat what was done before, with more relentless force,
so I was grateful for the hand that guided me into wider

freedom. Sometimes—often—I have needed the help
(another name for the love) of one of my Friends to see
me through, and I look back full of gratitude.

I signed on in a College of Horticulture, deep in
the countryside, and began classes in muddy classrooms
littered with compost and seeds. I learned about plants
and how they grow, about how to make ponds and paths
and arbours. I became practised in the skills of drawing,
in garden design—a form of divine geometry—and loved
it. Where had I been all my life? I had entered a new
world of the wonder of root cuttings, the cosmic dance of
compost, and my ability to draw, create pictures of
gardens of the future out of my own mind, that made a
place for all my new skills to live.

For the first time in my life I looked at the sky first
thing in the morning to gauge the weather. I knew by the
plants and trees around me what season I was in, and felt
part of the eternal circle of those seasons. I crumbled
earth between my fingers to feel its qualities, felt full of
joy when seeds sprouted, and in my first garden grew
twenty-two kinds of vegetables.

One of the first designs I created was for a large
garden in Surrey. When I finished the design I fell into
self-doubt. Sometimes I thought it was brilliant,
sometimes completely mad. I was certainly breaking
some of the rules my design teacher had given me, but

this might have been inspired, or it might have been beginner's folly. How to know? Who could I ask?

Well, it so happened that I read in a magazine that Sir Geoffrey Jellicoe, who was described as the most important landscape artist of the 20th Century, was re-publishing his book, *Jung and the Art of Landscape, a Personal Experience*. There he was, over 90 years old, and still creating landscapes, presumably with some kind of deep, Jungian cast to whatever he was up to. Well, I thought, sounds like my man, considering all my long fascination with the spiritual and the forces within our minds and hearts. Jung and the art of landscape. I was intrigued. So I took a chance, found his number and gave him a call. Amazingly, he answered the phone. I told him what was going on with me and my design, and how I needed a skilled eye to tell me if I was mad or talented. He was charming, and invited me over for tea. He asked; 'When would be convenient for you?' For *me*?

So I went up to his flat in Highgate, North London, and we talked, magnificently. We discussed art, gardens, Jung and the subconscious, the collective consciousness as expressed in gardens, and we looked at the art of his peers like Ben Nicholson on his walls and he questioned me on what I could see in what they had done. I'd never done anything like this in my life, it was great. I was in another world.

Then we looked at my design. I felt like a child at primary school as I unrolled it in front of his experienced eyes. He spent some time looking at every detail, noting every nuance, seeing what I hadn't seen myself. Then he looked at me over his glasses and said, to my surprise, 'This design is on the fringes of true art.'

'Eh?' I said, shocked. 'What? Art?'

Jellicoe looked at me sharply. 'Didn't you know you were an artist?' he asked.

'No', I replied, feeling awkward and uncertain, 'it never crossed my mind.'

'Well, well', he said, peering at me over his glasses. 'What did you *think* you were?'

This was the question of a life. What did I think I was? He considered what I thought I was to be far less significant than what I was, and that clearly I had no idea of what or even, perhaps, who I was. And what I was appeared clear to him, because at some level I was what he was. My goodness, he put me in the same species of human as his friend Henry Moore.

I left the old master and walked round Highgate as high as a kite. What a difference there was between what I thought I was and what I was! And we hadn't even touched on my other identity, the tricky issue of gender that had plagued my life. But again, the question was the same; what did I think I was? But on that magic day, all

other identities seemed of lesser importance when
compared with being an artist. I'd been lost for most of my
life in a wild garden of ideas about what I was, identities
taken from someone else's shelf, a sort of one-size-fits-
anyone way of making a life. When Jellicoe told me what
I was, the slipper fitted, and I felt like Cinderella going to
the ball.

The essence of all this is the power of recognition.
Jellicoe recognised me for what I am—in one essential
way—and he was such a figure of awe to me that his
opinion over-rode all my own mindsets. I sat in a tea-
shop in Highgate and tried on a new identity, like a new
suit of clothes. I am a woman artist. My heart leapt in joy.
I wondered why it can be that we are made to fit a suit of
clothes that doesn't fit, as if it is some kind of somber
duty to deny ourselves, as if what we are is unacceptable,
not quite good enough, a weight to drag though my sorry
life. How much of our wonder and talent can be lost like
this. How appallingly sad it can be to lose ourselves in
this way, and how heart-rendingly common it is to see
that loss on the faces of so many people, even more as
they get older and apparently further from the fulfillment
of their ancient dreams.

From that point on I made gardens from the depths
of me, according to what rose from inside. I had faith in
the promptings of my own inner being, and at the same

time began to understand great gardens, how the blend of line, texture, plants' leaves and stems, and colours, water, light, reflections, geomancy and love, come to touch us in the way they do. It's not just gardens, of course, it's life itself.

When I was leaving Jellicoe, I asked him if I could see him again, and he answered, what for? You got what you came for. From this point, in the art of landscape I had confidence in my own eye of understanding, from recognising myself after being recognised by another. Gardens are not just gardens, they are a way to expand consciousness, to open our minds. They are vast works of art that we can become part of by entering them.

The touch of one master told me to do gardening, the touch of another master gave me recognition of an essential part of me I had never known, because I never looked. Recognition is an essential power that changes lives. I'm writing now because many years ago one teacher recognised that I had talent, and that touch stayed with me down the years, like a seed that would one day sprout.

Another work of art I created out of that same creative source was the person that a friend called Persia, and this went on at the same time as making gardens, one form of creativity feeding into the other. Gardens kept me on the ground; they are unyielding in their demands for reality, being present and real, being obedient to the time and the place and the nature of plants, water and earth.

Jellicoe told me a story about Henry Moore, to whom Carl Jung once wrote. Jung tried to tell Moore about the forces in archetypal significance and symbolism of his art, but Moore didn't want to know. He didn't want his mind to be sparked off and start telling him about what he was doing before he did it. This would just get in the way of his artistic creation, the way minds do, as they deny the gorgeous dynamic force of the inner being, the Self, the wider and deeper consciousness that is what we are.

In this way, I had the faith to create myself once more, having once done this as a child according to the expectations of parents and society around me, but now according to the less logical but far truer urgings of my heart. This is the way I found that it's not just the courageous art of making gardens that is the great choice, it's the courageous art of making ourselves.

12

First the Stomach

All my life I had been terrified of the consequences of
tearing off the mask of the boy, that I had been given as a
child, and had been wearing ever since. That mask was
my protection, my identity, my normalcy, no matter how
much it wasn't me, no matter how much it hurt. It was
something like wearing the wrong size shoes but not
knowing anything else, so living with discomfort was
nothing much. It's how many people live, after all; you
can see it on their faces. It's normal in our world not to
be who we are, it's socially acceptable, in fact it's often
socially desirable.

Nevertheless, the day came when I could stand it
no more, and I removed the mask. I stood there feeling
naked, almost without a skin, I was so open and
vulnerable. My previous fears of the consequence of

being real to the people in my world were guesswork; you never really know what will happen till you do it. As it happened, it was both better and worse than I imagined. Some people cannot abide having their fragile certainties rattled, cannot bear the evidence that the foundation of their being is built on sand; if mine was, so was theirs. Reaction can be intense. Gender is assumed, without consideration, to be fixed, certain, immutable. It is the foundation of our identity in the world, the first identity we are given, and the rest of what we think we are is built upon it. Make my gender uncertain, and what am I? This question appears to be true more for men than for women, in my long experience. Perhaps the male ego can be more fragile than the female, more created, more easily threatened.

There are as many ways of experiencing this essential shift of identity; as many as there are people who undergo it. Mine was seen through the lens of long spiritual practice and understanding, which gave it context and meaning, made into yet another means of coming back to myself. I had a solid base beneath the turmoil of change. The feet of my being were in the calm water beneath the wild waves of the stormy sea, and this unchanging base held me together.

The first stages of the sea-change of my life were about dissolution. There is no spring without a winter. It

seemed that all the structures of my life fell to pieces, as
if the identity I had lived was the cornerstone of my life;
take it away and the rest collapses. This was a very
educational experience, a way to witness death and birth
without dying.

While I was in the middle of my meltdown, the
winter of my life, I had great company to see me through,
not only in the form of my Friends who I will love forever,
but also in more distant friends, who wrote to me in their
books. At that time I read *A River Sutra*, that marvellous
book by Gita Mehta which has the magic touch of being
written from the heart. In it there is the story of the Jain
monk. The Jain religion is little known outside India,
little known to me. It has something of Buddhism about
it in my mind, and is well known for its scrupulous
respect for all forms of life, even to wearing masks to
protect unfortunate insects from our mighty inbreath.

This tale is of the prized son of wealthy man
turning his back on all of his inherited wealth and power
and position, and renouncing the world in the way of a
Jain monk. The afflictions he would be taking on himself
were recited, and to my ears they were very familiar. You
will be a social outcast; you will be insulted; you will be
hounded; you will depend on strangers for your most basic
needs; they will despise you for their weakness that
imposes on their charity; you will be heartsick. I

recognised my own experience in this. I differed from the
young man renunciant in the story in that I didn't choose
this way directly, although it was the consequence of my
choices. In other words, it was my choice, simply made
less consciously. The effect was similar, with similar
benefits; take away the unreal, no matter how comfortable
the cell, and what you have left is the real. It may be tough
at first, but in time the void becomes full of sweetness.

I can understand from this experience the fear we
have of loss. At that time I appeared to lose almost
everything I thought was me; my family, my home, my
spiritual community, my name, my money, my work, my
self respect, my hope, my pride. I was pared to the bone,
but I still existed, I still lived, I was still myself. But I know
what it is to be without a home, without money, with
friends not wanting to give me a bed because who knows
how long I might stay? I know what it is to be cold in my
own home. I've had the good fortune not just to taste but
to feast upon the desperation that lived in my heart, and
in the hearts of many, but which is kept at bay by our
attention on the ten thousand things of life. I was given a
space on the floor by a friend who had nothing himself;
he had nothing to lose, he'd already lost it, so there was
nothing to fear in what I reminded him of within himself.
What a treat to know these places of desolation within
myself, in what other way would I have found compassion

within myself too?

It can be remarkably easy to lose so much. I was astounded at the fragility of the house of cards of my life. I fell swiftly, with gravity, down the black hole. It is far more difficult to climb back up the slippery walls that do nothing to stop the speed of the fall. But it all works out in time, with grace and effort. I now know I need little, which is a great freedom. I have visited the place of chaos and uncertainty within myself where none of us have identity, no place to call home, and it's really what we all are, where we live, and it's wonderful to become friends with this place in me on the way to becoming myself.

Lucky me. I can see why the Jain monks consciously set out to lose everything, especially their sense of self-importance. It brings me back to nothingness, nothing to hold on to, nothing to be, and the amazing thing is that it's just fine. In fact, it opens the doors to what I always wanted.

As for all the stories of my gender and dissolution, re-creation—well, like all the tales we tell ourselves about our lives, the cast of the telling is more important than tale itself, or the truth of it. All memory is flawed; selective according to the story of our life that we have come to believe is true. That life story contains and shapes every tale we tell. In fact, they're all untrue, as in the end there is nothing but where I am. Right now I am sitting on a bed in the middle of the night on the side of a Welsh hill in springtime, with a tiny cat leaning up against my arm, purring. Everything else is movements of mind, and I'm not listening to that mind when it begins to spin its webs, so I have no story unless I decide to want one.

I know, from having experienced the loss of the foundations of my life—money, home, warmth, companionship—that before we focus on the spiritual, the heart of what we are, first of all we must be well and safe, fed and watered. Before we even begin to have interest in the spiritual side of life, the heart of the matter, we must have a home, food, shelter, love, kindness. I thank my little home every time I return to it, thank the windows I can see through, the water in the taps, the shelter from the rain—honest, I really do—because I've been without and I know what I have.

From this experience, I know well that what I am writing about these days is not yet for everyone. Many of us need simple kindness, a home to call home, health, money in the pocket, warmth, friendship, nourishment for the body and mind, then we can begin to move out of the mind and into the divine. It's a constant choice to remember compassion for those who do not have my good fortune.

As I once heard it stated, before anything else, before God, first the stomach.

13
How to See in the Dark

Some years ago, when we lived in Japan, we used to take our holidays in South East Asia. We'd buy a ticket to Bangkok, pack a bag full of those lovely yen that grew on trees in those good old days, and wander off into exotic landscapes, travelling where we fancied. It's a long time ago now, but the memories still make me feel warm with love for the mystic orient. We felt like two kids who had run away together to the ends of the earth, scampering off hand in hand into the magic wood. It was lovely not to be enchained by the expectations that had defined ourselves and our lives back there in the home sweet home of England.

One night during one of our travels I was fast asleep when a voice in my ear woke me suddenly.

'Wake up, wake up,' she said, with an urgency that

snapped me into life.

'What is it?' I asked into the warm, thick, tropical darkness.

'Where are we?' she asked, voice full of panic. 'I don't know where we are.'

We were in that odd place that belongs to sleep in the wee hours of the morning, half awake, half asleep, somewhere between dreams and the so called realities of our waking lives. The room was completely dark, shuttered tight. It was warm and smelled vaguely of the east. We could have been anywhere in any one of the countries of South East Asia that we wandered round in. I sat up in the dark, and tried to remember, but something in her mindset and panic in a world without light had infected me. 'I don't know where we are,' I replied. 'I can't remember either.'

For a while we sat there in bed, clinging on to each other in uncertainty, and tried to work it out. Our normal daylight world seemed a long way away, remote and unreal. We backtracked in our minds, made the best of attempts to be logical, but in that inky darkness in the middle of our dreamtime, nothing made sense. For a few long minutes, we felt foundationless, and that in turn made us a touch desperate. Who are we if we don't know where we are?

Still, in the end we worked out where we were.

Penang. We smiled happily, now we were sure. The world which had seemed chaotic, formless, and had filled us with uncertainty, one of the faces of fear, instantly fell back into its normal obedient place. We yawned and, feeling secure once more in knowing where we were, fell back to sleep. Only to wake up in Java.

The scene in the night, which seemed real at the time, and the normally real world, remote and intangible at the same time, had reversed themselves. The obvious reality of a Jogjakarta morning overrode uncertainties with one look. But there was one aspect of all this that has made me feel uncertain about reality ever since.

It isn't necessarily the truth that makes us feel secure; fantasies can work just as well. What we *think* to be true can be as comforting as what *is* true, sometimes even more so. It's not so different from thinking a rope is a snake and feeling fear, only backwards. Don't you just love the flexibility of the conscious mind?

This is another of those insights that can make the world wobble, if we are willing to look at our own, current forms of feeling secure. Here's the question; are we seeing in the dark? Is the foundation of our sense of security made up out of fantasies and dreams designed to make us feel better, for a while? Does this really work? Aren't these fun questions? I love the way I find—if I dare to look, right at this minute—that there is that element of doubt in where I think I am, even if just for a passing wobbly moment. Take a further step and there may be doubt about who I think I am as well—maybe this is just another fancy, maybe I'm someone completely different, maybe this is just a dream. I remember the story from the Chinese sage, which sums this up neatly.

One upon a time Chuang Chou dreamed he was a butterfly, flittering around from sweet flower to flower, supping on nectar, completely and in all ways a butterfly. There was no other awareness than that of a butterfly, with its own ways and wants and sense of being. After a while he woke up, and there he was, Chuang Chou the man once more. Now he does not know if he is man dreaming he is a butterfly, or a butterfly dreaming he is a man. There is, of course, a distinction between the two, making one or the other into reality. Penang or Java, woman or man? But which one is real, is it both or neither, or is the critical point being that which observes the distinction and the dilemma?

Here we are back with uncertainty, insecurity, one of the gateways to being more free. The truth is that we never really know, no matter how well we've constructed our castles, how pretty the numbers look in our bank accounts, how the value of our house is holding up well, how our pension will see us through to a happy end, how certain we are in our identity.

I'm one of the lucky ones; I've got nothing. Let's correct that; I'm one of those who *knows* I've got nothing. What I mean by this is that at the depths of us all, when we wake up in the middle of our nights, all manner of dark doubts easily emerge from our fertile minds: Where am I? Who am I? What's this life all about? All this darkness in the darkness is usually kept tidily out of sight by our ceaseless attentions on our lives, on the dramas that make us feel we are real, that we exist.

Once more, all of *what* we see depends on *how* we see depends on *where* we are seeing from. Although it's great to have lots of stuff, houses, cars and so on, they only really matter at a pretty basic level of vibration. I know well how vital it is to have the basics of life handled; food and warmth and shelter simply have to be handled; I've been over the edge and know. When they aren't, the focus is on money and houses and food, to the exclusion of the more elegant aspects of our lives. An obsessive focus on money is a drag on life, shared, oddly, by the very poor and the very rich, at the point on the circle where they meet.

The place we see from varies according to many factors, but the essence is the same. Do you believe in the thoughts, the words, sentences and stories that are told to you by yourself, not only in the dark of the night, but also in the light of the day? It's back to the jungle, those

wild jungles of thoughts, ideas, imaginings, longings, fear,
of needing to know—when we never will and it doesn't
really matter anyway.

If you wake in the night and don't know where you
are, it's usually OK. The best thing we could have done
all those years ago in Jogyakarta was to simply snuggle
down and go to sleep, wait till the light of morning and
be delighted by the magic of Java. Am I a butterfly or a
wildebeest, a woman or a man, in Java or Penang? The
conscious present moment we were living was warm, dry,
well-fed, comfortable, with the best of company providing
love. Stay with that, the immediacy of the present
moment, and all is well, or at least not so bad. The
troubles began, as they always do, with the mind just
needing to know where the body is, or needing to *think* it
knows where the body is. Fantasy upon fantasy, unreality
casting spells, creating worlds of darkness in the darkness.
It's all just dreams, waking or sleeping.

If we make the choice to be present, here and now,
we don't need to know where we are, or what we are, or
who we are, we just are, and that's more than enough. In
writing this, following the way I am producing these
words—without planning, trusting that the next word,
the next sentence, the next pearl in the chain will come
and make some kind of sense—I went back out of the
words emerging from God knows where to the silence of

where they come from, the void inside. The instant I make the choice there it is again, that delicious sense of my own Self, my own presence, my own being, which is so high and sweet it can see in the dark.

14

The Eye in the Mask

Masks are strange things, with odd powers all of their
own. Slip on a mask and something changes in the ether.
Strange powers emerge from places we didn't know we
had in us, and strongly affect not only the person who
sees the mask with its glittering human eyes, but also the
wearer. It's all a bit creepy. I once tried on a variety of
masks, egged on to take risks by someone who was a
master of the art of masks. Her collection was mainly
African, and they were not safe at all, even to look at on
the wall, never mind to become the bearer of. I noticed,
amongst other things, that I could be affected by the mask
in a way that matched the face I was wearing without
having seen it first. A fierce-looking mask made me feel
fierce. A clown face made me feel comic. How does this
work? What comes first, the mask or the character? Is

our destiny in our face? Or does our destiny create our face? It's easy to be frightened by the uncanny effect of masks; they can make us nervous because they work with primal forces that we are not familiar with.

We really don't know what's going on beneath the surface of our perceptions, and it can make us feel uneasy when we realise that we don't know much about what shapes our worlds. Let me help you to wobble. The place of unease, uncertainty, is the starting point of choice, so it's where we want to be, where we begin. Just be not quite so sure of anything at all, even your name, your gender, your story—and through that crack comes fresh possibility.

The truth is that we all wear masks, we all create our appearance, using our faces, our clothing; and this extends into the way we walk, stand, eat, enter a room, speak a phrase. These are the familiar masks, which fit with our identity and our place in the world. Slipping on a radically different mask and its effect may well trouble us, especially when it appears to be at odds with what we have come to think we are. All of this helps shape our worlds. More often than not we are unaware of the nuances of what we do, despite their effect on the world around us. Here's the big point for me; without being aware, we don't realise our options. This then means we have no choice but to follow down the old tracks, wondering what went wrong.

These appearances are all self-made, engineered by us, even though we may think that how we come across to others has just happened, like the shape of our nose, or the colour of our hair. But become acutely aware of movement, the way we hold our bodies, the slight turn of a mouth, or a shoulder, the shift of weight, the way we use our hands, and we begin to see that everything is a message, a statement of who and what we are and how we should be treated. It's complex and done in a thousand details, and we read it all in others like open books, even though we may not know we are doing it. We are all actors strutting our stuff on that Shakespearian stage of life. Professionals know it, and know how they do it, and with this awareness can consciously manipulate their effect on others, as do politicians or salesmen—to a degree. They are rarely aware of the deeper depths of our being, the world down the rabbit hole, the undersea world of our minds, that we are wandering in here. Most of us prefer to work in our zone of comfort, and the principles we are looking at here are too deep for comfort, for most of us. But we are usually unaware of all this, and can be locked into sending out communications that create an effect we don't like, but feel helpless to change. Help! I'm in a cruel, cruel world.

Masks are about identity. When we look at

someone, we see messages about who we are looking at, and these messages are a mixture of conscious and unconscious, aware and unaware, in both in the giving and the receiving. The unconscious part is the most interesting for me. It's where the power lies, it's the hand in the glove. And similar to hand puppets, the masks summon credibility, even though we know they aren't real.

It's the unusual, the black sheep, the person who doesn't fit well that can show what works for all of us equally well. With the unusual, we can see the principles of how we work as if on a stage, lit up and easy to see. What we are seeing is us, no matter if we think what we are seeing is nowhere near where we want to be, still we are seeing ourselves.

In the theatre we can see the conscious assumption of mask, identity, persona and role. It isn't everyday life that reflects theatre; it's theatre that reflects life. As for individuals, we have much to learn about ourselves from some of the great stars who have created an image, a persona that touches something deep in those who see and feel it. The image was created, taken on, then sometimes became more powerful than the person who created it. Charlie Chaplin comes to mind, with his immeasurably powerful little tramp, who emerged from a collection of bits and pieces; the tight jacket, the baggy pants, the funny shoes, the cane, the moustache. Their combination took Chaplin over, changed him, created millions of fans and dollars. This image touched many people very deeply, and I still don't quite know why. I wonder if Charlie did.

My particular fascination is with Mae West. She created her character out of another collection of bits, including the parody of woman from a drag artist, and the sight of a tattered prostitute dancing with a sailor on New York's east side, with a bird of paradise feather swaying in her hat. One savage irony is that Mae West, who couldn't let go of her own creation, Diamond Lil, or even Mae herself, was parodied by the drag queens who helped create her, even before she died, when it was said that others were then doing it better than she.

Mae was a woman of sharp intelligence, and her comments on her Diamond Lil persona and herself within it are worth listening to. What she said isn't just highly relevant for our age of celebrity obsession, it also means you and me and our own created personas, our own masks of life, worn over our own bright eye. What worked for Mae West, what chained her to her own creation, works the same for you too. She wrote these lines, and you could try inserting your own name in place of hers, to see how you feel about your own creation:

My basic style I never changed. I couldn't if I wanted
to. I am a captive of myself. It or I created a Mae
West, and neither of us could let the other go, or
want to.

This makes me feel terribly sad. It's not the
artificiality of the mask she wore for the world, it's the
fact that she was trapped by it. She was attached to her
own creation, more bewitched by her own creation than
anyone, and the tension between her two identities when
in fact there was just one was tearing her apart. It's not
reality that's the problem, it's the persona and its mask
creating a world that traps us, denies us ourselves.

What all this means is that, more often than not, we
think we know what's going on with our identities and its
masks, but we don't. We may be unaware of much of
what creates our identity to ourselves and others. Back to
the boy on the beach, to a young person who has created
an image identity to keep family happy, with an identity
in the heart that was at odds with this. So the boy who was
a girl had a mask for the world to see, and an identity that
was radically different from that mask. The untenable
tension between the two was what blew her mind. Once
more, this radical experience is an example of what is
true for many. Does the mask someone else designed for
you truly fit? As the eye in the mask, that glittering eye,

well, that's the reality of the person shining through. If we know this we can choose to look for that shining eye of the living person just like ourselves in every appearance that comes our way, then we can recognise reality that exists in that moment between us and in who we are, and meet, heart to heart, soul to soul.

It's not too hard to do, in fact it's easy and completely natural. It happens all the time.

15
Oh, Viridissima Me

I am writing this in the hills of North Wales which were a part of my world when I was a child. Yesterday I was down in the Caffi Florence, the café down at the country park at Loggerheads where the coffee and cake are good, when I realised I must have first come there more than fifty years ago. How could this be? How could so much of my life have passed? I came with my parents, then I came as a schoolchild to the camp at Colomendy just over the road, many times over the years. Is that child me? Just because I have memories, however vague, of the world through the eyes of a child, does that make the little kid into part of what and who I am? What I appear to be keeps changing, so it can't be me in the deeper sense; child to adult, boy to woman, young to old, gardener to writer. Nothing remains the same, except something does, and that is what or who sees the changes and wonders about this changing world. The child saw the same river at Loggerheads as the adult sees, and in this case both the seer and the seen have not in essence changed.

What has also not changed is the love of the greenness of this place, which I never lost for a moment, but sometimes didn't live. When I began to create gardens in the early nineties, however, I was once more returned to the place of nature, plants, weather, rain, belonging.

The overwhelming green of this place, the fresh mint green leaves on the trees, the darker green of the carpet of wild garlic with its little white flowers and garlicky scent on the breeze, the green of the hills, shining wet, the green river burbling through the trees, all this was imprinted on me long ago as the feeling of my own paradise in this world. Now I'm back, childlike in another way, following one of those odd spirals in time that I live, tramping over the hills I scampered over years ago, same place, evolved same me, different world that is the same. The same eternal rain I am watching fall right this moment in bright sunshine, dappling the surface of the great heart-shaped pool I dreamed up and made, is the same rain from the same sky. So close I feel to this place right now that I have a warm, inviting sense of wanting my body to lie in the earth here when its time is done. I love the idea of it merging with this particular earth.

My sense of time has changed along with
everything else, with the passing of time, and it's not just
being older. With the shift in my own state of mind, state
of Being, state of heart, this is the same world and a
different world, all at the same time. It's back to the boy
on the beach, the boy in the hills, the boy in the green
pond; the woman on the beach, the woman in the hills,
the woman in the green pond. Delightful paradox once
more, containing with love the apparent opposites, in
myself and in my world. The solution to the problems is
to go beyond them. Stop asking the questions and there
is no need for answers.

Recently, I was trying to grasp a concept of the
collapsing of time. My mind couldn't do it; this is not the
kind of thing minds are good at. They are wonderful at
their real work, being our servants, dealing with the things
of the world, bus times, taxes, the way to Casablanca, but
they end their uses at the gateway to the temple, where
the guardian lions of paradox sit. Then, trotting down
the stairs in the library in Brighton, I got it. You can't
work it out, you have to just get it. Lose faith in the mind
and all its complexities and limitations, and move a few
steps higher, where you find insight.

Nevertheless, the insight can be part-expressed in
words. The words, as in poetry, are a guide to the feeling
and the insight, and, hopefully, they won't make complete

sense. What I saw was this: the past exists now only in my mind, as in the memories of my childhood along the green river, my life as a boy on the beach, or, more recently but still past and gone, talking to my mother on the phone this morning. I can tell this is true because the moment I turn my attention from those memories, pictures, feelings, and look out of the window where the sun has broken through once more, lighting up the immediate incarnation of the Viridissima Virga—the ultra-green branch from the song by the ecstatic mystic Hildegard of Bingen—that past has gone. In fact, as I write, the sun has vanished once more as the moments of time keep moving on, and sunshine is just another memory.

Take attention, or interest, away from the past, and it no longer exists. It's something like watching channel no. 4 on TV, then flipping to channel no. 3; it's still there somewhere, but right here it no longer exists.

The future exists only in imagination too, and is another creature of my mind, which can only create its tales out of what it knows, which is memory. This is the place where my fears lived and caused me all manner of anguish, as my unrestrained mind cast its fears upon a blameless and non-existent future. Neither past nor future exist outside of my mind. The moment I got this, I became present once more, immediate—and the light of the world, of heaven on earth, shone bright. Time had collapsed. Sort of. Even that is another play of words and ideas; how can time collapse if it doesn't exist? Which, of course, it does—I'd miss the train if there was no time or I didn't believe in it. There, once more, is sweet darling paradox, containing both opposites with tender love.

Which brings me naturally to the nature of beans. In the conservatory here we have climbing bean seedlings growing in pots. Soon they will graduate to the poly-tunnel, then in July they can go outside. Remember this place is 1200 feet high in the Welsh Hills, so cold and frost can come late. Three days ago, I decided to give the baby beans their own sticks, as they were beginning to wave their dear little blind snouts about, looking for something to twine around. Almost immediately they found their canes with their acute sense of touch, and began to twine and grow upwards, which is what they are born, or germinated, to do. I could almost feel their joy. Oh, I have a stick all of my own! With enthusiasm they spiral upwards. It's their green nature.

Within the little beans is the green power of this world which, on this hill with constant rain and long days of light, is exploding silently around me, each leaf, stem, flower, tendril bursting with the ecstasy of sunshine melded with green, which has the power to turn sunlight into leaf and branch and bean, the form in this world of the ineffable green Goddess.

What I can see is mine, more than that, it is me. All
of my perceptions exist within me. This dazzling world
all around me is nothing less than me. In other words,
what I can see *is* me. The force of spring is within me as
much as within the green hills. There is no separation
when I am in myself like this, I am nothing less than the
Viridissima Virga that I see. Outside of time and memory,
in the constant heart, I make the choice to be the
Viridissima Me.

16

Now is My Body

I am now in the third part of my life. The first two are done; I have lived my youth, and family life as parent, my single child is grown, now I am with myself; more than at any time my life is my own. I am deeply happy with this changing body that is the single measure of my age, which is reckoned from the time of the arrival of this body in the light of day, so age is age of the body. It has nothing to do with the mind or the spirit. My dear body has served me well for many years; it's healthy, fit, and lithe, it digests well, it's reliable. I have looked after it, and it has looked after me.

In the Indian system of contemplative yoga that has been the foundation of my spiritual life, the body may be considered no different from the mind. The body is seen as a denser part, the mind a more expanded part, of the same unity. So, to live well, we need to take care of both, or, more precisely, the single unity of our being. Minds and bodies are as blurred in their distinction as are male and female, right and wrong, all opposites that define a world for a mind of limited scope.

We all know that our minds affect our bodies, and our bodies affect our minds. The two are intertwined, as they are in fact one and the same. If we drink too much, eat too much, eat poor food, take to many strong drugs, we feel bad. If we feel depressed, or angry, or stressed, our bodies reflect this, in tensions, pains, all the way to severe illness. The body simply expresses disharmony in mind and feeling with physical sickness; it is one and the same thing.

Sometimes, however, we are just ill. The body is simply how it is, and the single problem is our minds creating tales of discontent with current reality. Earlier this year I had a long bout of 'flu. It came and lingered for weeks, and with the weakness that comes with sickness, my mind tried to tell its old tales of how wrong it was that I was sick, that I had better things to do, that I never get ill these days, and other tales of self importance. It wanted to find the psychological importance of this imbalance, making the illness wrong in some way, controllable by will, and so on.

After a little indulgence in this resistance to illness,

the particular form of present reality I was living, I
surrendered, and other imaginings of how my life should
be were cancelled. As long as I was denying where I was,
I was worse off than I needed to be, so I made myself a
nest in my warmest room and pulled down inside myself.
That day it snowed deeply, and that white shape-changer
of the world added to the mysterious inward turning,
isolated from life feeling that the flu granted me.
Sometimes I need to stop turning my energies and focus
on the outside world, and be with myself in a form of
chrysalis, while the forces that created me as well as
snow and time and 'flu did her gentle work in my body.

So often these days, with our partial understanding
of the deeper nature of bodies and their problems, we
spend all manner of time trying to understand where our
illnesses come from; is it in our minds or stars or karma
or troubles in past lives? The mind, the mind once more,
eternally busy eternally embroidering the simplicity of
what we are living right now with complexities that lead
us away from where we are in this moment, which is the
single truth.

The Buddha had a story to tell about the insistence
we humans can have in needing to understand the source,
the provenance of our distress. A man on the battlefield
was struck by an arrow through his shoulder. As his
friends ran to remove the arrow, the first necessity in

recovery, the wounded man stopped them. Don't take it out until I know the name, the rank, the family, the caste, of the man who fired the arrow, he demanded, bringing on his certain death through dense pride. Better to just take out the arrow, of course, why bother with the obsessive doings of the constant mind? Things haven't changed too much in two thousand odd years. Still we can be reluctant to let go of our arrows, or the pain we hold in our bodies and minds, until we know more about where they came from, why, who caused them, and on and on. Our modern religion of psychology can enjoy this, feeding into the fascination we have with our pain and our past, and less interest in forgiveness, being present, and freedom.

Of course, when we're sick, or cold, or hungry, or homeless, or lonely, when we are not so strong in body, the mind has greater freedom to take over and have its way. The two are interconnected, they are the same stuff. This means is that I need to be more vigilant, even more on guard, even more ready not to believe the stories of doom and despair that come out of the darkness when I am not so strong.

So when I was sick I found goodness in being still, disengaged from my busy world, in a womb of dark warmth. Perhaps this was another form of pre-birth— will I be someone else soon, again? It's a nicer kind of thought, but it's still a thought, and these days all of them are suspicious. Who cares about speculations about what something in my body means? In the end, under the endless thoughts there is no meaning at all. I found this tough at first, when I discovered the nothingness under my mind, that there was no story that counted, nothing going on at all in the heart of me. It was something like being at home in the evening without television to fill in the void of time, the perceived problem was just being with myself. To be precise, it was not the empty time that was the cause of my small or large distress, nor was it being with myself. The problem was being with my mind and its tales of woe, troubles, fear, discontent that could now run free in open space. In the same way that I used to distract my son when he was a little child, to take his mind off immediate distress with a picture book, or a new game, so television, books or radio can distract me from the mind, give me some kind of passing relief, but no solution.

Better just to be here, and with practice find that being present without the critical, painful, complaining, dissatisfied whining of the mind has its own subtle sweetness that beats high drama, if we are willing to let go of the dramatic tales that seem to give our lives form and meaning. My body is too big, too small, to fat, too thin, it's old, it's diseased, oh me, oh my. Like most people like me, I've been there, done it. The way to go was to be present, be alert, be with and in my body no matter what. Whatever came or went, the one thing I could be sure of was that being present, conscious, out of the manic mind and its stories, would not only keep me feeling well in the heart of me, it would also be the best of foundations of recovery or re-creation, if that was my destiny. But who wants to speculate about that? Destiny, fate, karma, hell, I don't know, but I do know being here in bright presence, and more and more I know that this is what makes for good futures.

What's more, I've had the good fortune to find the great joy in my body that comes with scrupulous attention. My way of giving to my body, that which carries me through life, St Francis's Brother Ass, is through practising the yoga of the body. Lucky me. I have spent years now opening and re-aligning, being acutely with every nuance of what my body is and does, how the blood and the nerves and bones connect with each other in one great dazzling system, as intricate and balanced in wonder as a galaxy, or a flower.

When I am focused absolutely on my body as it moves and flexes, watching its wonderful intelligence and tending it all as its keeper, my mind is still, and with stillness comes joy. In other words, I don't have to stop and discount what I may consider imperfect in this body of mine, I can move on and up and take the gift it is as a means of being the only here, the only now, the single choice, as always.

Now, at this time in my practice, I'm finding new ways of counteracting the strange strains and imbalances that my imbalanced mind brought to my body. I am standing on the earth with consciousness of my toes and heels and bones and arches, then from this present and conscious planting on the earth I follow the spirals up my legs into my open hips, then up my spine, my shoulders, my neck, and the way my head sits there, looking at the world around.

Over time, I have become more acutely aware of all the tiny inflections of this body, minute angles, ways of holding shoulders, hips, angles of neck that are subliminally visible to everyone around me. I send out messages to the world with my body, but until I became conscious of them, there was a barrage of what was being sent and what was being seen that neither I nor the receiver knew much about.

How much better it is to know, to take the choice to be here and now with acute attention and miss little or nothing, present with our lovely bodies, our lovely lives, no longer lost in the jungle but flying free overhead. The way for me to fly is to choose to be on the earth, surrendered to gravity, present and full of life.

17
The Speed of Mirrors

I was down in one of our giant supermarkets, wandering through the clothing section. Aimlessly, I turned a corner between two aisles, and noticed a woman approaching me down at the end of the long row of clothes. She looked oddly familiar, but I couldn't quite place her. I looked away, she looked away. I looked back, curious, she looked at me, curious. I felt edgy, uncomfortable, a bit threatened by her attitude. She was a strong, tall, confident-looking type and, feeling a touch uncertain, I looked directly at her in a challenging way. In the moment she gave me the same challenging look back I suddenly realised I was looking at myself. The mirror I was being reflected in was so large I couldn't see its edges, so I didn't realise it was a mirror. Intrigued, I stopped and looked at this strangely familiar woman standing in front of me. 'Well,' I said to myself, 'so this is how you look to other people. Nice to meet you.'

It was a fascinating experience, which revealed so much of how my perceptions work. It was clear that when I look in a mirror, something other than simple reflection goes on. On that day, in front of that mirror, I stood remote in a special zone of seeing while the supermarket buzzed away all around. I looked at myself with interest, seeing the image of myself as if through a different set of glasses, or through someone else's eyes. I half expected the scene to suddenly flip back into normal vision, the distorted one I clearly made when I looked in a mirror, but it didn't, it stayed with me. I was in yet another state of consciousness, in another place in myself, and from that seeing another world. The person I was looking at was definitely myself, but quite different from the normal me in the mirror, more like the person other people seemed to see when they told me what they saw, and which I never quite understood. Their view of me was, of course, more flattering than my own. For sure, for some reason, we tend to see something lesser in ourselves in the mirror, we often paint ourselves in darker colours than are true. Such is the tendency of the mind.

I guess it was like seeing someone's photos of me, which they introduce by saying: here's a nice one of you— and I cringe. How can they think this is a nice one of me?

What are they seeing? Are they just being kind? Do they love me so much they are seeing a fantasy of me? This means that when I know it's me when I see an image of myself, something happens. I don't see reality, I don't see what is there before me in the mirror, I see something already in my mind. Or maybe something in my mind alters the image before it gets to me. There is a swift and expert hand at work, like a conjurer, altering images with an expertise I don't even begin to notice. The hand that performs the tricks is, of course, my own, but I am unconscious of doing it. If I became conscious of how I did it, could I then change to make it more of what I would want to see? In other words, how much of the world as I see it has been created by how I see it?

The implications here are staggering. If my own secret-from-myself instant-editing suite can create an image of myself in a mirror that is not what is seen by others, without me being conscious of it, is my world nothing other than a creation of this part of my mind? It's OK to see this works a bit, affecting details, but when I think of the way this works and the way I am not usually conscious of it, I wonder how much of my world is created by the way I see. It's not what you do, it's the way that you do it, as the old song says; it's not what you see, it's the way that you see it.

Another incident comes to mind. I lived in Japan

for years. Japan was home, it was normal. One day I was travelling by train into central Tokyo on the Chuo Line from Kichijoji, where I lived. It was the middle of the day and few people were travelling, so we all had seats. I was sitting there in a typical train traveller's spaced-out state, idly watching the city pass by, stations arrive, doors open and close and so on. Then, at one station, the doors opened and a gaijin, a westerner, got on. For a moment I was shocked. I was looking out of my own face, so I couldn't see it, all I could see were the normal Japanese people spacing out on the train in their own way, so this red-haired, sky-tall, nobbly-nosed, long-limbed, gangly great gaijin galumphing into our neat and trim, harmonious Japanese world came as a real surprise. My goodness, I thought, look at that! Then, a moment later; Good Lord, is that how they see me?

The answer was; not exactly. When I was first in Japan I was noticed, people responded to my difference more often, but with time the reactions diminished. I began to be more invisible; I slipped easily through Tokyo without making waves. What made all the difference was not so much how I looked, which wasn't so different, but in how I used my energy, my attitude, my subtle body language, the way I didn't look at people. It wasn't how I looked that mattered; more important was the way I was seen, and I had a clear hand in this. What could be merged

with Japanese society was merged, I belonged as an
outsider, and this change made my world change too.
How I was seen depended to a great degree on something
subtle in how I put myself across, but if asked, I would
have found it hard to say what that difference was.

In some way, similar to seeing a different image of
myself in the mirror, which showed me how I projected
much of what I saw of myself out onto light and shadow,
I'd temporarily joined a kind of Japanese vision of my
own kind. Perhaps I'd flipped into their collective
consciousness and in consequence their way of seeing,
because I'd been there so long and was so at home that
part of me had merged.

The big question, of course, is this; if what I see is
a projection, a fantasy of myself when I look in a mirror,
where does this end? I just know that this doesn't end with
my visions of myself, because I'm just another object to my
awareness. Taken to a logical conclusion, it means that I
project something of myself out onto everything. What's
important is the way I see the world; this is what shapes
it and gives it meaning. The World is the way you see it.

Once more I can feel my certainties delightfully
wobbling. Is this world not as real as it looks? Blimey, does
that mean that I am not as real as I thought? Uncertainty
once more, evidence of the emergence of the possibility
of truth. If the world every one of us sees is different even

slightly, and we don't know we are doing it, what is real? Is anything real?

Back to Einstein and levels of consciousness. Real is what you think real is, and that depends on where you're thinking from. What's more important than what we perceive, which changes all the time, in form, in meaning, in how it looks, in a thousand ways, is the perceiver. Whatever happens, however it looks, it's still me who is doing the looking.

Take this step, make the choice to step back from the action, from the movie of life, pull back from the screen, and here I am not changing at all. When we look in a mirror, something very fast happens, so swift that we don't notice, but it's no different in the rest of life. It's all smoke and mirrors, and it's a lovely show.

18
There is Time

By the slowness of our eye
And the quickness of God's hand
The world exists

The Mahabharata

The eternal cry in this funny world I live in, my home, my place, which has faults and darkness as much as it has light and goodness, if that's how I want to look at it, is that there's no time.

What this really means is that there is not enough time to fit in all the ten thousand things we need to do. We feel pressed from all around by the hands plucking at our sleeves, like beggars, all wanting us, wanting our attention, our knowledge, our skills, our money, our benevolence, our love, our time.

It feels as if there is simply not enough time to do everything in one day, one month, one life, and we commonly feel exhausted, stressed out, abused, and with that we lose track of ourselves. When we lose track of our own being, who we are and where we are going and why we are living like this anyway, we lose the whole of the point of life and it becomes dry and desperate.

When we think that there's no time, what it means is that we've become trapped in our little minds, again. If I feel that familiar sense of panic, stress, loss of control, then I know it's time to check in back home again, which means coming back to myself, checking out of the spin of the mind. Remember, there is no time to worry about, there is no past, there is no future, there is nothing but here and now, and when I look at this blade of time I am surfing, in scrupulous immediacy, there is nothing to be worried about. It's not so much that all will be well, which suggests that right this minute isn't, it's being aware and present enough to see that all is well right now, the foundation of a future of nows. The future is made out of the present, of course, so all I need to do is be in the good present and fear not. It takes practice. And it takes faith, but faith comes with practice too.

All of us know that there is another way of living than being in trapped in the wheels of the mind, with all its dark tales of past, future and present, because all of us have experience of being free of it, if even for a short time. It could be at night when we are all alone, it could be when the plane takes off and our life is left behind for a while, it could be when twilight settles and its peace comes over us, or when our children have left home, at last; whenever it might be, it's come to us all. Just for a while we find ourselves in a clearing in the jungle, and often don't notice that it's a clearing in our minds first and foremost, that the source is ourselves, that we are not victims of circumstance at all, circumstance is a victim of us.

It's the boy on the beach again, and the simple truth that freedom from the ceaseless activity of the mind is available, if we remember, if we want it. That tale of mine from the beach way back in my own story is a tale of extremes, and it may seem that there are only two ways to be; in misery and in bliss. But we all know that there are as many states of mind as there are moments in a life.

With each state of mind, none of which ever last long, come different perceptions of everything, including time. In fact, how time seems to you is a fair measure of where you are on the infinite sliding scale of states of mind. A way of looking at it is that we operate at different vibrations, that they are fast or slow, or the frequency is higher or lower like a radio, or our minds are contracted or expanded. The higher or faster the vibration, the more expanded our vision and the more we can see. This is the high road, the way to go from here, the choice I have when another way seems real.

We all experience the way the world, or our perception of it, changes according to mood or feeling. When we feel miserable, the world is a gloomy place, our external reality is unpleasant, no matter if we are in paradise. This is evidence of a low vibration level or contraction of mind. When we are very contracted, say when we feel suicidal, the world seems hostile and divisive, hopeless and dark. Once I took a prescription drug that threw me into the darkest depression, into a place in which suicide seemed a logical way forward. I came out of it when I saw a glimmer of love through the darkness from those around me who loved me, I could not deny it, even in the depths of my own deepest darkness. At that point I began to rise from my own depths and in time all became well. There it is, love, the highest vibration of all, as the sure way up and out, if we are willing to make that our choice.

When we shift from a contracted state of mind to a more expanded one, however it's done, even if we shift just a little, then the world seems more cheerful, people better natured, and the beauty of the world may be restored. The ultimate expansion is love, so love is always a way. Even a little has the power of truth behind it, and the application of a little love to ourselves can heal many a wound.

Between the extremes of suicidal depression and enlightened love—and the boy on the beach moved from one to another in an instant, really outside time—there is an infinite range of frequency possibilities, all of them in different colours. We don't have to fly, to set an impossible goal of immediate enlightenment as yet another way to ensure feeling bad. It's fine to shift just a little, there are many states of being, and with practice we find they are ours to shift. The variety of states is staggering, impossible to imagine. We move through a range of these frequencies, vibrations or contractions of mind, every day, every hour. Not only do we feel differently when we expand, we also perceive differently. When we are contracted our vision is limited, when we are expanded our vision is wider. It's like climbing the tall tree in the jungle; the higher you go, the more you can see, and time changes its nature too, it becomes more friendly, softer, and provides the space to let us solve the riddles of our lives as they are right now.

This is what Einstein was talking about when he said that problems are never solved at the level at which they were created. We have all experienced this, when we get all knotted up over some issue that seems insoluble, then give up and relax, take our white-knuckled hands

off the wheel, and there is one of those moments when
we simply *see* what's going on—rather than understand—
and the solution is clear. It's wood and trees again,
moving out of the jungle, from thought into awareness.

This is the beginning of the way to go, this is the
choice, when you get the knack of choosing, of high road
over low road. It seems that our society is dedicated to
thinking and talking what we think, preferably in endless
meetings, or with friends who agree and disagree with
how we think, a mass of opinions to create a jungle of
thought to get lost in even deeper. My head spins at the
thought, as beliefs and attitudes and powerplays go round
and round and go nowhere. You pays your money and
you takes your choice, this is one way of living. But there
is another way, and it's not about working it all out
discussing it, living within the mind, being addicted to the
force of words, sentences and stories, none of them real.

One of the ways that different levels of contraction
or expansion, low frequency or high frequency of mind
change our perceptions is with time. When we are
pressured, we can easily get contracted, start shouting at
the kids, kick the cat, scream at the husband, and omigod
look at the time, there's no time for anything, we're late!
When we are relaxed, feeling fine and cool, centred in
ourselves, one thing tends to flow into another, the kids
are just doing what kids do and they're getting there, the

husband has his own life to lead, the cat is safe sleeping on
the best chair, and there's time on hand. What happened?

In the Indian philosophy that has opened many
doors for me, the worlds of our perceptions are created
through pulsations of consciousness that flash out, vanish
and reappear, that the universe is re-created endlessly, so
quickly that we don't see it happen. Again, it's like the
frames of a movie, all the stills that run into each other to
make movement, create the illusion of a world on a
screen in front of us.

Our eyes blink; the world vanishes. Our eyes open
again, the world re-forms. Even on this level, our worlds
are created and vanish thousands of times a day. The
world in which we are living right now is not the world
we were living a moment, a day ago, there are subtle and
not so subtle changes occurring with every breath.

All that changes is how we see it, and that depends
on where we see it from, how open and expanded are our
minds, our consciousness. Before we can choose to shift
our level of consciousness, we have to know that we can
do it, we have to know that there is a choice, and this is
what I need to remind myself of, time after time.

I make my world, *how* I see it makes *what* I see. A
constant reminder comes with my current perception of
time. Am I pressed, anxious, is there no time for this, no
time for that, no time for myself, no time for love? Ah,

then something needs shifting, not in the world *out* there but *in* there, in me. I need to stop, come back into myself, become conscious of my body, the moment I am living, take a deep breath, and unhook myself from the clutch of at least a few of the thoughts that I am hooked onto, and find myself once more. The relief is always profound, and I know that I've made it back home when I find once more that, in fact, there is time.

19
Great Expectations

For so many of us, the love we have lived with for many years can turn with mysterious cause into poison, sweetness becoming bitterness and rage, closeness and trust vanishing, and we may be left with estrangement and despair. How often is this strange transformation the tale of our close loves? It seems impossible that years of warmth and tenderness, the deep trust that is the sweetest comfort of all, can vanish and then show a dark belly of mistrust, separation, anger and all its relatives—without us knowing what went on, or why. And it can happen suddenly, as a storm can arrive from nowhere on a summer's day, or so it seems. Truth is, there are always movements in the subtle worlds that presage such storms, it's just that we are often not aware of them, or avert our attention from oncoming tragedy.

My experience of the art of relationship counselling, which aims to avert breakdown, focuses on expectations, both known and unknown, conscious and unconscious. The hidden power of our unmet expectations is, it seems, a common cause of embittered endings of closeness and love. As with icebergs, the visible is less of a problem than the invisible. What is beneath the waterline, that which is unseen, is far larger, far more dangerous, and at the same time hidden from sight, so is apparently not there at all. What? Me? Expectations? The visible parts of the icebergs of life are similar to icebergs in the ocean; what we can see is only a guide to what lies beneath, where the true danger lies.

As I worked at seeing my invisible expectations, making conscious that which was unconscious, I was amazed at just how much there was of myself beneath my radar, how many complex emotions within me created the circumstances of my life. I thought I was the innocent party, the wronged, the ill-treated, the victim of a cruel, cruel world. How wrong I was, how little I knew myself. As the mists of my ignorance began to fade, I was able to see something of the way my expectations had created an impossible standard for life itself to meet, not just my nearest and dearest, and existed only to make another person wrong. Oh, and to make me right, of course.

It's that old devil mind again, creating another

person over the one in front of me, unreality over reality, accusations on the innocent. The expectations I found hidden within myself existed intangibly as feelings and thoughts, and at the time I was locked onto them, invisibly, because I thought that they were true. This is how we make our worlds, create like a conjurer's trick what we think is reality out there in our sight, but is in fact no more than the reflection of our own attitudes, convictions, and the emotions of suffering we love so deeply. The outer story is nothing other than the inner story. We don't need anyone to fabricate our dramas; as with a movie, all we need is a screen, which in our case is anything, or anyone, apparently out there in our ever-shifting world. When I look back with the detachment of the years, I can see I just loved it, adored feeling wronged, in the same way we love to feel scared in a horror movie. It's what we pay for, these ghastly soap opera dark feelings, as I paid for my emotional indulgences, but in a different coin from the entrance fee to the cinema.

There is a story I heard in India, about the dog and the bone. A dog was given a bone, and, as dogs do, it began to chew and gnaw away at it. The more it crunched and bit, the more the sweetness of the dry bone filled the mouth of the dog, and the more enthusiastic it became in its gnawing. But what the dog had not noticed was that the splinters of bone were cutting its own gums, so what it was tasting and relishing was its own blood. This is how I lived with my feelings, so righteous, so justified, so wounded, so real, so delicious, all my own life-blood.

The game in the end is all our own, there's nothing out there really, it's all in here. And it goes on and on, repeated and repeated as we read the same story that we wrote a long time ago, day after day, never tiring. My relationship with my mother is fine now, for example, although it wasn't. How she has changed! But when I remember how all things with my father changed when I found gratitude in my heart, how he changed before my eyes, I begin to wonder. Who changed first? Who made this world of mine? If we create even a bit of our experience, in a way we didn't acknowledge or were unconscious of, how much more can we shape and colour? Just how much of what we perceive outside is nothing other than our own inside? As long as we keep a bit for ourselves, keep something back to blame on something else, we are trapped.

Once upon a time in my life, I thought—felt deeply—that I was in essence, wrong. In fact, to back me up in this hazy way of thinking that is more feeling than thought, someone near to me once said; *you're absolutely wrong*. That's what friends can be for, of course, to tell us what we want to hear, to confirm our identity and validity of our living dreams, or nightmares. I was a constant disappointment to other players in the drama of my life, who defined themselves by being disappointed. Disappointment only comes to life when we have an expectation that is not met, of course. The line that I heard time and time again, because it works so well, setting expectations which would never be met, went like this; *I thought you were going to ....*

You can fill in the dotted line with anything you fancy; make more money; be a real man; go to church; get enlightened; exercise; paint the hall; be an example to us all; be stronger; stay beautiful; get a job that I can be proud of when I tell the neighbours—as long as it's unreal, and is a standard that will never be reached, it'll work just fine.

Now it takes two to tango, of course, so in this case the dance needs someone to state expectations, which is the 'I thought' bit, the mental projection that exists only to diminish reality, and another to feel bad because they don't meet them. But the critical point for me here is that what others expect only touches us if it matches an expectation of our own for ourselves. It's a sure way to misery for everyone, and it's clearly what we want because it's certainly what we get. All of this exists as reality at a certain level of thinking, attachment to a certain state of mind that permits such lunacy to be considered real. Step out of contraction of mind, open your eyes, and there's nothing there to feel anything about, because the thoughts and feelings simply cease to exist. Hello, reality.

It was only after I'd moved on in myself, had stabilised at a better state of mind, that I looked back and wondered what that game was all about. Why on earth would anyone, especially me, do a thing like that? Hell, the agonies, the genuine pain of never reaching a fantasy destination that someone had about what I should be or do, which secretly matched my own lunatic unreachable fantasies. I never once looked at this with sense, because I was too locked into the madness. As usual, the problem lies with our unexamined assumption that the thoughts, ideas, expectations—and so that are the soon—are real. What would we be without them? Who would we be without the drama of our own life?

It reminds me of having lunch with a fine and wise man some years ago, when I lived in Tokyo. There was another man eating with us, and he couldn't stand the sight of me. His loathing was tangible, so much so that we talked of it openly because it hung heavy over the lunch table. Our wise man asked me if I realised this had nothing to do with me at all. No, I said, I didn't, I suspected it was based on some reality. Well, he said, you'll suffer until you realise it's all him, there is nothing of you at all in his feelings, his perceptions, his reactions—in truth he is loathing himself. He was right; now I know it had nothing to do with me at all. The tracks within my mind that still held the misery of believing I may be worthy of loathing, have vanished. Where did they go? How? But where did they come from in the first place?

No answers from me, these days I can wait till the question vanishes when my state of mind changes. All I need to know is that if I approach someone with an idea of what or who they are, and depending on the power that I have over the person, then this idea, thought, image, expectation, entraps both the seer and the seen.

What's wonderful and liberating is that once we don't want that game ourselves, don't want to play the part of the person who suffers under the wild imaginations of someone else, first of all it has no effect on us, and second, it tends to vanish anyway. When I realised that the moment I would no longer play the game of great expectations, no-one tried it on any more. I had to kick myself when I realised that they never were the source of the problem, it was always me. The love of my parents, the love of anyone, was always in my own hands.

So here's the magic mind, folks, the dazzling power of our own lovely minds. What all this comes to is this; there's nothing out there, it's all in here. There is nothing that is not within our own consciousness, including other people. We're all one complex of conscious mind, and it's the jungle unless we get higher, open up, so that the hooks and eyes that trap us in thoughts that make our worlds are released. It's not the thoughts that are the problem, actually, it's our attachment to them, our attachment to being contracted, defining ourselves as wrong, as needing to be told that there were expectations that were never met. Unhooking them from the zillion eyes is like peeling ourselves from the Velcro of the mind, and this is freedom, otherwise known as liberation.

Imagine we are looking down on ourselves from heaven, and we can see all the people busying around like ants in a nest. Look how well they work together, the harmony is amazing. While I was watching my world one day, not from heaven exactly, but from one of those upper decks on the 27 bus where spiders sometimes live, I noticed this harmony in the streets around, and thought of the difference one person whose mind has gone astray can make to this world of ours, one nutter on the rampage, and how rare it is in my safe world that anyone at all visibly errs from harmony. We all buzz along in a safe and warm shared resonance, in amazingly close harmony as we live our days.

How we see other people comes from ourselves, what we see is how we see, and how they see us is what they see. It's like a host of mirrors. Expectations, thoughts that rise up and take shapes like the wrong lenses in glasses, shift and change that world of ours, they make it unreal. If we want to live in a better world, if we want to be happier, if we don't like feeling like outsiders, the source is not out there in others, getting them to fit into the straightjackets of our expectations, because they never will. All we need to do is to be here, be open, see how the machine works at a level of thinking that creates a world of disharmony, and not want to do that anymore. Expectations exist to create disappointment; that's it. With practice, knowing this, we can create our world according to what we really want. Truth is, I always did, I just didn't know it; perhaps I didn't always know what I wanted; now I do it's not what I want anymore.

OK, to remind myself: time after time, because I need reminding—by myself, or anyone else. No expectations, walk the line with eyes open, here and now, notice the tiny flickers of emotional or intellectual response to anything, unhook from it consciously and be here. See everyone, everything, not through the dark glass of great expectations, but straight and real, face to face.

20

Why, it's Almost Like Being in Love

What a day this has been
What a rare mood I'm in
Why, it's almost like being in love

Cole Porter

Some years ago, at the sort of age when I really did know better, I fell in love. I imagined that this could never happen to me, that I was cool and above such things, but happen it did, all in a single moment. I didn't have a good time of it, as it seemed to me to be mostly painful, intense, full of longing and despair, because it had nowhere to go. But the power of it was astounding; it filled me night and day. I loved it and hated it all at the same time; it was wonderful to be so alive, so overwhelmed with feeling, with passion, and at the same time it was spoiling me and the rest of my life because I was taken over by the infamous madness of obsession. Nevertheless, something within me that had been asleep had woken up and roared. To have this part of me woken was essential, so I am grateful.

I'd read Robert Johnson and his Jungian insights into my own being, so I understood something of the nature of romantic love, in my mind, but sterile understanding was made irrelevant by the force erupting inside me. Reason was burned in a flash of fire. What I understood was what I had not fallen for a person, but had become hopelessly seized by the perception of an unlived, unfulfilled part of myself, projected on the innocent—well, not too innocent—object of my passion.

I was in deep middle age at the time, the age of discontent, the second adolescence, when the distant whisperings of our own inner beings that have been faint in our lives may begin to demand their own immediate life, no matter what the cost. The calling in me was of Aphrodite, the appalling force of the feminine power that had already taken me, but was still incomplete. There was no possibility of compromise; no prisoners were to be taken in this game, it was total surrender or nothing.

At that time I saw an exhibition of the work of

De Kooning, the Dutch painter, when I was in the
desperately uncertain place of dissolution of my identity,
and the inner force had not yet taken me completely. The
middle stage of any life transition, the teenage years for
example, can be hard, until we reach the apparent
certainties of the other side, to be questioned deeper at
another time. The paintings in one room, all somehow
similar, made me feel full of distress, and I had no
understanding of why this was. When I looked in the
programme to gain understanding, I read that the artist
regarded these paintings as of his own anima, the
feminine aspect within men, according to Jung, and, not
being able to stand the idea of these images being true
for me too, I fled. What did this mean? I wondered if my
subconscious was like a set of those Russian dolls, with an
anima inside my animus then another anima within that,
an animus within that, and so on. Where would it end? It
felt as if the essence of my being was vanishing, and I was
right.

    In regards to my obsession, this all pointed to the
solution to my anguish not lying in the beauty and power
of the woman outside me, but within myself, which was
far more terrifying. I had sheltered within a created
masculine persona as a kind of defence, which was being
subsumed by the feminine, step by step, bite by bite, cell
by cell. I was scared to death of losing myself completely

with what was emerging from my own being. It was safer to stick with the illusion of it being a force, a person, a perception, outside of myself, but that story was wearing thin. It was time to face my own inner wonders, to find that the phantom lover was myself.

So here we are again, wandering in the subconscious ocean, where all manner of forces lie, like monsters that are out to eat us up, till we realise that they're just us, and we are far more than we ever knew—if we take all these magnificent powers as our own. The denial of what we are is nothing other than believing in the mind again, as it runs wild and creates worlds, or personas that don't exist, on top of those that do. This is Maya, illusion, the world of thoughts which are so much the cause of suffering, sometimes in the form of self denial that always hurts, no matter how we pretend we're used to it. We are what we are, and if we can simply be here and now with ourselves, all is well. But this is so often so hard to do; the fear of being ourselves is so great that it takes time, a lifetime, and so often it never happens at all.

I look back in my own life and I can now see how I put together the mass of ideas, perceptions of what was right and wrong, how I should be, how I should live, what sort of work I should do, and on and on. It wasn't just what came in the form of words spoken to me and feelings imbibed, until all this became my reality, my being, who I was, my destiny, my cage. It was me taking this raw material and knitting it into an idea of myself that became reality. The good news is that what I knit I can un-knit, just as with a sweater, and the yarn can be used to make something more stylish, more me.

When I saw someone who was a reflection or projection of who I had denied in myself, the passion of recognition blew me away. The way to go, so hard to do when so much of what we are led to believe is outside us, outside our control, our destiny, our hope, our love, is to turn away from the object of our passion and look for the same within ourselves.

It seems to be the nature of the human being that we can more easily accept the darkness within ourselves (what we think and feel is wrong), than the light (what is great and good), so we can get to see it in others and pine. Is it somehow inherent in us to feel right when feeling pain, somehow unacceptable to be have greatness, power, freedom and enlightenment as simply who we are?

A great woman from my own life once said to me; 'You are either surrendered or not. If you are, you know it.' How wise she was. Surrender may sound like a passive defeat, a slumping into weakness, but it isn't. Surrender means accepting the force of our own true nature, who we really are. Surrender is an act of being open and real to what and who we are, what life is. It's literally a revelation.

The problem was that being myself, way and beyond what I thought I considered myself to be, was far too much to take on board; it was unbelievable. The inner being, the Self, which is simply what we all are, can seem overwhelming, and it's often easier at first to see its qualities in someone else, a lover, a guru, a teacher, a myth. But one day it has to be turned around and accepted; in the end there is nowhere else to go, no other way to go from here.

In my long road back to my spiritual beginnings on the beach in Formentera, there has only been one issue, one block on my way back home, and that is attachment to my mind. Is there anything trickier than handling the mind? But this is the great game, delving deep into the ocean of our own being and sorting out the wordplay of the mind, what we thought we were, and in the end it's where the joy lies.

Falling in romantic love was another step on the way back to myself, if I was willing to take it on board, if I was willing to let go of my habit of seeing the outside as something apart from myself, my excuse in powerlessness. Oh, the wonder and beauty I see outside myself, how distant, unattainable, nothing other than a measure of my smallness and how far I have to go. How tricky the mind is, how much sense it makes to itself to justify its own power, make real its own world.

It takes time. It takes time, even though it might seem as if all is possible in a moment, so we need to be compassionate to ourselves. Everything we see, and everything we fear and love, is nothing other than ourselves. And in the end the only way out is to love all of who we are, with the love of the mother who sees every part of the child and takes her without hesitation.

In the end I came back to myself, and I can't believe my good fortune. Here I am, the woman in the hills, writing away in the cool wet summer, in lovely solitude, weeks now all by myself. I have become that which I thought I loved in someone else, thought existed in someone else, because I couldn't face the power and the wonder of it being me. Now I am living my once unlived self, and it is a return, in a way nothing new, not really a surprise because it's so at home. Looking back, I wonder what took so long, but who cares, why bother asking, why not just be here now in this paradise of early summer?

And now I have taken myself unto myself, I'm looking out at the world of people and feeling easy and natural affection, warmth, forgiveness, interest, towards them. When we are who we are, it touches the same place in others, so it spreads like a divine virus. It feels great, so light and free, so present, so ecstatic, so simple, nothing fancy at all. Once more, nothing new here, nothing special, nothing we don't know already. We've all

touched the centre of ourselves, we've all been touched
by the centre of someone else, even for just a moment,
but that moment is unforgettable.

The days I live are nothing other than that moment,
unless I forget to remember what I am and let that mind
of mine play out its fantasies. Life is then sweeter, with
no plans, no future, no past, everything here and now
with no need to understand.

In fact it's not so different from being in love with
someone else, with a great and significant difference.
Instead of it being outside myself, a projection of my own
being that I've not yet embraced and taken for my own, it's
been turned round and embraced and recognised as me.
With this I have all the sweetness of love, the passion and
aliveness, without the pain that can so often accompany
the illusion, as the illusion fades and empty reality takes
its place.

Oh! I gasped as I embraced myself and sweetness
overwhelmed me. Making the choice to turn back to
myself as all that I long for fills me with love and passion
and joy, why, it's almost like being in love.

21

Magic for Beginners

I was taught from an early age to cast spells. It was part of my growing up, it was expected, natural for kids in the suburbs of Liverpool. We were taught by our parents first of all. They taught us the basic techniques, then we added complexities and sophistications from others, for example the teachers at school or our friends. One basic trick we learned was how to make people do things they didn't want to do. What you do is to see them as being not quite right, or even completely wrong, according to a standard you make up yourself, if there isn't a convenient assumption on the shelf. Once you've got that going, which is easy—because everyone's doing it and it's completely natural—you start looking for evidence of their shortcomings in what they do. Using the magic word 'should' is evidence of doing it right. This person should leave his job, my child should be more focused, my sister should leave that feckless boyfriend. Should is the magic word that tells us we're up to no good. But still, you'll find it easy, it comes naturally, everyone's doing it. What empowers this way of acting, makes it invisible and makes it work very well, is being concerned, wanting the best for people, caring enough to be honest. This is a legitimate way to find darkness in just about anyone.

Now, here's the magic, and this is where quantum physics enters the picture. If you don't know what quantum physics is, well, you should. I don't know much about it either, but I don't let that get in the way of talking about it, in the way I've read other people do in books they have written, which is a perfect example of how to write a book, that I've taken on board. It makes life more interesting when you don't know everything about what you're talking about. It is, as Jung wrote, 'the charm of the new, the fascination of the half understood'.

So, quantum physics—not even half understood by me, therefore way more fascinating—says that the behaviour of the observed depends on the attitude of the observer. In other words, all we see is what we expect. But when you're dealing with people, not just tiny particles (and this is where the magic really comes in) you don't just see people behaving according to your attitudes and expectations, they actually do behave that way. What we see in people isn't just an illusion, as in what you see is what you get, it becomes reality.

Now it does help here to have social power, for example to be a father or teacher or boss to produce magic effects. Being a husband, or wife, or lover, may be even more effective, come to think about it. Perhaps it has something in it of the need to be loved that weakens us, opens us to the projected power of others, makes us clay in their hands. Will you love me if I act to fulfil your dreams?

One of the best examples of this is with children, because they are so malleable, so ready and open to be shaped. As can be the sensitive, delicate, or kind. The parent insists on the child being a clumsy fool and, although they are well co-ordinated and smart with their friends, around the parent they drop things, say dumb things, and behave according to the parent's expectation. Give them time and it's what they will become. This is the magic; they feel something happening to them as the spell takes hold and their nature changes to fit some 'fluence in the ether. It's the same at work, or with our friends, or lovers when we descend from the first frisson of love which distorts the vision and makes us see angels in flawed humans. What we see in people affects the nature of that person, we can diminish anyone we have power over. It's pure magic.

The magic effect of our vision of another is endlessly amazing. I had a friend who was a talent scout and promoter of models. She just kept her eyes open and found young women, girls really, in stations and coffee shops, anywhere, and would see some quality in some girls that she recognised immediately. They might be dressed in an old sweater, unwashed, clumsy and too young to know anything, but my friend could see their potential, see what they had, see the fine statue in the lump of marble. So she introduced herself, took the girl off and washed her, dressed her, made up her face and took some pictures. The photos were always amazing. The girls looked beautiful, elegant, sophisticated, and they were astounded, entranced, bewitched and beguiled by the secret images of themselves. What power female beauty has. Funny thing is, said my friend, give them a year and they became beautiful, elegant and sophisticated. What came first, the beauty or the vision? For sure those girls never would have become elegant models without the recognition, but neither would they have been spotted without a certain quality that could be recognised.

So the magic can work both ways, it can destroy or create. But notice the essence; we affect the world around us with our minds, what we think, and the world around us affects us with its mind. It doesn't happen physically, in ways we can see and touch, it happens with forces that are invisible, intangible and work at a level of our being that we are not normally conscious of. This is why it seems like magic. That's why it *is* magic.

We live in a giant complex of unseen forces that mould and shape our worlds, and they go from the seer to the seen, from subject to object and back. It's so complex that our ordinary minds simply can't grasp it.

Most of the time, people are unaware of the totality of these powers and forces. We live our lives so engrossed in our minds, our stories, our dramas that we see as if looking down a tunnel, or between blinkers. Step up one or two notches in state of mind, take a breath, make that essential choice to let go for a moment, turn off the mental noise, and we can feel what's going on, we can become acutely aware of the slightest breath in the conscious forces within and without. It's great, who needs TV? Then the doors to perception are open, and we can see the wonder working within and without. That which was always there and rarely seen is visible, and is all our own.

And now we know about magic, the interplay of forces within and without that make what we call the world, we realise that our part is a leading one. In fact, we are the centre of our own world. Close your eyes and it goes away, it ceases to exist, open your eyes and it exists again. Then remember that we blink thousands of times a day so the world is coming and going, every scene slightly different, millions of times a year. At the centre of it all is you.

You want a world full of beauty and goodness? Well, you have the magic power, you can choose this consciously, if you like. You want to have talented and sweet friends? See them as talented and sweet, then, so you have nowhere to go to find what you want.

I am a writer now because at the school where I felt so lost, and which considered me not quite right, one teacher recognised my ability to write. He cut through the mass of distress and loneliness of the poor kid who was thought of by many to be different, not right, and gave me the gift of recognition. It lit a spark in me that is a fire today. Now there's magic for you. Thanks, David Aitken.

It's not hard to find something in anyone to recognise, to acknowledge, to praise even, and watch that fine goodness swell in them. As we do, well, we feel that same goodness, talent, wisdom, within ourselves, because you can't see what isn't in you.

So in the end the magic is recognising ourselves, seeing the goodness, the talent, the divinity, in ourselves—and with that, changing the entire nature of our lives as we see the goodness, the talent, the divinity in everyone else. If we are ready to take a chance and go that far.

It's the magic choice that makes magic worlds.

22

Traveller,
There is no Path

Caminante no hay camino
Se hace camino al andar
from *Cantares* by Antonio Machado

I was driving home across the Downs, the range of
voluptuous chalk hills that protect Brighton from the
North. When I am coming home and see the Downs
ahead, I know it's not far now, then I sweep upwards
onto the curves and swoops and sky on the Downs, and
the road that curves and swoops through them. These
hills are soft and rounded, female hills, like a host of
sleeping women covered in green, and when I get to the
top of them I can suddenly see the sea glittering in the

distance and it's almost time for tea.

While I was driving the other day I let go and flipped into the Zone, the Self, the Awareness behind my mind and its thoughts. It's that place where consciousness changes and time seems to slow, everything seems easy and flows naturally from one thing to another. People talk of this state of being in sports, in war, and in love, and all of us know this state of grace from some time or other in our lives. I watched my eyes as they switched around, looking at bends and the way forward, the sides of the road, passing cars, amazing in their skill, and my hands on the wheel doing the steering without the slightest effort from me, simply knowing all about what to do and how to drive. My body on the seat was just sitting there and within it my breathing, no doubt my heart beating, all of the vast conglomerate of what is loosely called me, at work in intricate harmony.

This body is a miracle, so skilled, so intelligent, and this, along with an intelligence that lies behind all of this complexity is what drives my car. As well as all the other cars on the road, all skilfully zooming round, their people maybe imagining they are driving, the way they do, the poor things. It was like a gigantic ballet through a divine set. All I do is to set the destination, but even that might be coming from somewhere or something else. Perhaps I am deluded once more in thinking that it's me who is in control of anything at all, so even choosing my destination may be nothing other than my destiny.

And here's the greatest wonder. If something wonderful other than me is making my body alive and driving the car, is it also running the rest of Life? So the question comes to be not just who is driving the car, but who's driving this life? It's the Big One, the question of questions in yet another form.

In this space of grace, it's as clear as day that everything is a divine harmony, that there is an intelligence that does not just drive this life, this world, this universe, but *is* this universe, and all I see and know is nothing other than this greater Being, call it God if you will.

Driving cars is no different from any other action in life. There are two ways of doing anything—from the sense of being someone who is driving, with all things in my control and, in consequence, my responsibility, and being the constant and untroubled observer of it all as it unfolds in intricate perfection.

In the state of Being, there obviously is a Plan, as spring opens, the sun rises and sets, my next meal will be there (lucky me), my birthdays keep coming, and the time that doesn't exist in this immediate moment will be filled with activities until the body dies off at its appointed time. So why not have faith? Why believe in the doubts and

fears of our little busy minds and have the overwhelming
need to control what has never been in control?

Coming from the Self, there is no path, because it
only exists in a fantasy projected out into a future that
doesn't exist. The entire sense of this revelation came to
me from the wonderful poetry, heart and mind of Antonio
Machado, poet of the mystical, in the seventies when I was
living in Spain. One of the many lines that have echoed
in my mind ever since are at the beginning of this piece:

> *Caminante, no hay camino, se hace camino al andar.*
> *Traveller there is no path, you make your path by*
> *walking.*

This is the magic point of choice that I live every
moment of every day, the eternal fork in the road which
time after time offers me The Choice. Is it the high road,
or is the low road? Old habits die hard, and still my mind
whispers at me to take its way into such traps as regret,
despair, resentment, ill-will, because I loved the dark
feelings of their dramas for so much of my life. But I am
rarely tempted now, if ever, because the high road is now
my committed way. I've had enough of soap operas,
enough of self-indulgent dark emotions, self-pity, jealousy
and rage. I aim to live well, be truthful to myself, not
because of some high moral ground I take, but simply

because I have had enough of suffering, and I have come to love the lightness of freedom.

So how come there is no path and there is a path all at the same time? Well, it's another of those apparent paradoxes, made of those concepts that are what the mind is, and which only exist in relation to their opposites. There is no future, there is only this immediate divine moment, from which we look at the ever-changing wonder of consciousness that is our existence, and the changes of which we measure with time. There is no path, as Machado wrote, it's only footsteps on the sea.

It all depends on where we look at it from, from which level of consciousness. When we go high, there is no path, there is just here and now with no plans, no futures. But when we live our lives from where most of us live them, it seems that there is a clear pathway, we have a past and a future, and the present moment hardly exists.

But it isn't real. Reality is watching my body drive my car from its own intelligence, knowing that there is something which is not my thoughts and imaginings which not only drives my body and my car, but drives my life. We just keep walking, one step following another, as a kind of breathless act of faith; in the end there is no other choice.

Einstein talked of an optical illusion of consciousness that created difference and gave us the impression of being separate. This optical illusion can be removed with the right prescription of the glasses of perception. It's a kind of waking up and seeing what's going on, when we are lost in that same old jungle of the mind and, with some act of grace, rise above it to see that everything is a single magic, ruled by a single benevolent consciousness that is in essence our very own selves.

So where do I go from here? Oh, I don't know, I don't even know what I will write next, I just sit here and see what comes out of me, or through me, or what is appearing on the screen of this little computer. Where does all this stuff come from? All I know right now is that if I'm writing about going outside and beyond the mind to live a life, which is what it's all about, there's only one way to do anything, certainly only one way to write something like this. Stay balanced in the moment, become acutely here, don't listen to my thoughts, don't believe them for a moment, and watch what happens. Look, books get written, lives get lived, cars get driven across the Downs, I go to the supermarket, I rest when I am sleepy. Something in me knows what is good for me, and what is good for me is good for everybody when we come from the right place.

There is no path, that's just another idea in the mind. Life is the single act of faith, the choice, a stepping out onto the sea.

23
If it Ain't One Thing ...

The price of freedom is eternal vigilance. Turn your back and the mind is spinning one of its old familiar tales, and once more we're in the drama of life according to me. I broke a cup the other day, a nice one which wasn't mine, and my mind immediately started in some seed form to begin the thoughts and feelings of guilt, but I didn't let it. A friend told me a lie, and there was the temptation to make something of it, but I noticed and didn't let my mind involve me in that story either. It's raining again, another Welsh summer is on us. And for a moment today, the beginnings of the thoughts and feelings and judgements about the weather in this place and what that meant, started to run. But I caught it, ignored the temptation to play the game, again, and to find myself in another episode of the Persia soap opera that I loved, or at least

watched every minute of every day. After all, I am, or
was, the writer, director and star of that entrancing soap,
so of course I'd never miss an episode. Maybe it was just
another kind of addiction, which meant I didn't love it,
or even like it, I just couldn't let go of it. But now, thank
God, I have an option, I have the choice.

   I've read thousands of books, taken classes and
workshops, I've chanted the names of God for months of
my life, I meditate, practice hatha yoga, and in the end
what helps me, secretly, to keep me on track in my daily
existence, right here on the ground where I live, is very
simple. I no longer believe in my thoughts, my
perceptions, my past and my future, I don't give them
value, make them real, and let them attach themselves to
me. Everything is the same, in a way, made of the same
material, consciousness, and it changes all the time. What
I say to myself, generally in silence, as yet another thing
happens which might lure me back into the Game, is this:

   If it ain't one thing, it's another.

   I like it because it's kind of funny, not serious and
spiritual sounding, but to me it makes all the difference,
it really helps keep me on track during my days, as I'm
living this life of mine, with all its twists and turns. I break
the cup, oops, crash, and my mind, always eager for

contraction, immediately wants to involve me in thoughts and feelings; the traditions I was taught to believe in were self-criticism, fault finding or guilt. I know it so well that I could let it fly right now and start its work, but it wouldn't work, because I'm conscious of its ways, I'm detached from it, not lost and believing it's telling me the truth.

What it wants is to contract my attention, draw me down into a darker place, take the low road, and take a part in the old soap I loved to play in, same episode every day. It's like the pied piper, wanting to draw me away from myself, have me dancing off down the road to doom. Because what I'm committed to is being aware, awake, acutely in this moment, not deep into stories made up by my mind; my direction is clear, it's the high road every time. I want to live like this because I like to be open, expanded, conscious and light. I like my life to be sweet, I've become addicted to being free.

I notice the cup fall, oops, crash, the faint twitch of mind with its seed of thought I know so well, because I'm aware, vigilant, ready. I notice what's gone on, I'm aware in an instant of the cup and the crash and the mind, so this means I have a choice. Hm, I say to myself, *If it ain't one thing ... it's another.* Immediately I'm detached, the event is just another event, one of millions that pass me by. The most important practice, for me, is constant detachment, uninvolved, which means I'm here, present,

not off in some tale made by my mind, so I'm not a spider
spinning a web over the simple reality of what is here and
now.

It's a trick to keep my mind in its place, which is not
running my life. I feel it's a restatement of the Buddhist
concept of the impermanence of all things; all things
come, stay for some time, then go. Our hold on them
must be light, then we're free. I stand here being present
and life flows on, one thing follows another, change is of
the essence, suffering begins when we hold onto a passing
moment, or try to. In truth it's like trying to grasp the
wind.

Minds are minds like dogs are dogs; they have their
nature, which means they can be studied and understood.
The nature of minds is to create thoughts. They do it all
the time, it's how they are. If my attention is taken by
something, like the falling cup, or the friend telling a lie,
along with a slight sense of alarm or concern, there is a
gap for my mind to run into and begin doing what it does
best. Without discipline some dogs, some minds, will run
around causing chaos. So you need tricks to distract them,
discipline them, keep them in their place.

If it ain't one thing ... I start to say to myself, and
the whole game is put into another context. It's not so
serious, it's OK, just something else going on. Take it easy,
don't get involved, just be here and be awake and take it

as it is. Doing this keeps me aware of what I am, keeps
me here and now where it's always OK. The critical word
here is aware. I can't be aware and lost in my mind at the
same time. If I am aware, then the mind is something I
see, it's just another object in my consciousness, so I don't
have to dance to its tune.

It's all hooks and eyes, me and my thoughts,
desires, fears, loves, hates. The problem is we grasp hold
of them, hook onto them, make them real and important
then draw ourselves down into the dark emotions that
are the meat of the story that then covers reality.

I remind myself to be present, to sit when I sit, lie
when I lie, eat when I eat. Zen, it is said, is cleaning the
dishes and sweeping the floor. Nothing special, as they
say, we don't need to fly to the moon to find spiritual
inspiration, if we are aware and present, it's in every
living moment. I keep remembering not to forget, keep
vigilant, make sure I'm not in my mind, especially when I
feel hungry or tired or sick, because the price is too high,
not measured so much in the dark feelings of the low
road, but in what I deny myself in the way of delight,
pleasure in being alive, love, compassion and simple joy.

Then, when I'm here and now, present, aware,
something magic happens. I come into my own being,
and I am filled with what is now being called Presence,
which is full of sweet power. This is my own nature, what

is called the Self, the desireless state, because when we're in it, when we are it, we are complete and need nothing. I can feel it as a conscious force, and it's nature is ecstatic, full of joy. So unhooking from the mind and becoming acutely aware is another way to go, but it's far more than removing myself from contracted states of being that cause unhappiness, distress, loneliness and so on. Once unhooked and present, something truly wonderful comes to the fore. By becoming accustomed to this I have lost my addiction to the dark side, and have now become addicted to freedom and the rich, sweet feeling of being true, simply being me, that which was hidden behind the curtain of my own delusions.

Another of my own little tricks for myself is something I learned when I was driving in London. I was driving down Park Lane, and as I approached Hyde Park Corner, one of the busiest intersections in the city, maybe the world, a sense of despair came over me as I saw the bunched up traffic backed up the road. Then I noticed the despair, my old friend, and sort of shrugged inside and said to myself: *It'll all come out in the wash.* It's another way of detaching, and more than that, it's inviting the force that runs the universe so well, with the moon and stars in the sky, the petals opening on the flower, my heart pumping, on and on, for a lifetime, all working just fine without my interference.

I relaxed, sank back with relief into myself, then before my eyes in some miraculous way I found myself driving easily through the mass of cars, as if they had been parted by an invisible hand, and in no time at all I was free and somewhere else. This, to me, is the great key, the answer to my problems, not in what I do, but what I don't do. Let go of the wheel and my body drives; disengage from my problems, the knotty issues that are before my eyes now, and there always will be something while I live on earth, then something else begins to move. In the void of no-thought is the force and intelligence that creates the universe, moment by moment. Let it be, and it will sort out anything. So I say to myself, when I can see the temptation to take control, begin to fret, find things hard: *it'll all come out in the wash.*

Back to the gift of the Tao te Ching and the line that I learned almost forty years ago: *The world is ruled by letting things take their course, not by interfering.* To think of the unnecessary pains I could have avoided over the years if I'd let that happen. Truth is that now I'd rather not think like that; regret is just another trap, another hook to grasp an eye, if I want. See how subtle the mind is, how sneaky, how my mind knows just how to lure me away from my own being? Thanks, but no thanks, I'd rather be here, be present, be in the now, so with love, my mind, off you go.

My world changes on the spot when I disengage from looking down a dark tunnel of thought to a wide, expanded view, full of my own Being. No past, no future, just being here, lying in bed right now, writing. There's nowhere to go. Just wait for the next words to emerge, and look, here they are. What comes next? Who knows? Best to wait and see.

It's all about making the choice to move into detachment and grace, trust and surrender, surfing the divine moment, stepping out onto the uncertain sea and watching the path open up before us. As usual, nothing new.

24

The Look in the Eye

I always loved the Pointer Sisters singing *Slowhand*, one of those bittersweet songs that somehow tell the whole of the tale: *I saw that look in your eye, looking into mine, seeing what you wanted to see.* Don't we all know that one, say from when we were children, with fond adults seeing in our eye then projecting on us all manner of talents and futures of the kind they never lived? Or adults projecting on us what they need or feel they need to be complete. Or new or old lovers seeing what they want to see in us, while we know in some deep place that this can't last but hell, let's enjoy it while we can. What a curse it can all be, empowered by us because it's founded on our own desperate need to be loved.

Being bittersweet like this has two sides to it; I like that you're seeing what you see in me, which is sweet because it brings me attention, affection or another phantom of love, but I know it won't last because it isn't real, which is bitter. Still, as in the song, let's relish what we have while we have it, eh? Life on earth, folks, people seeing what they want to see, what they think they see, what they have been taught to see, but when they look at me, do they see me?

How many times in my life have I seen a look in someone's eye which tells me so much about where they are coming from, what their attitudes are, how open their hearts are, and with that how they see me, which is rarely even near being true. I know that when someone looks at me, more often they are seeing through some odd lens which makes me, in their sight, into what I am not. How often we simply want to be seen for who we are. Recognise me, I'm here, I'm real, I'm me! No matter how hard we shout, in fact the louder we are, the less we're heard. I'm here, beyond and behind all I show you and all you see. Even though it can suit us at times to be seen as what we want to be seen as, it's only fine for a while. In the end reality always comes, no matter how lovely the honeymoon, but no matter how we fear it, this reality is always best in the end.

Me, I was a funny kid. There was something not quite right about me. My mum says that the school was concerned about what was amiss, and asked was it bad

company? Was I eating well? All seemed OK with my
friends and my food, so they were mystified. It was none
of these things that was wrong, of course. The secret truth
was that I was secretly living a gender that was not my
own, and it gnawed away at my soul. Not being ourselves,
having to be something different than we are always hurts,
no matter who we are, and when that pretence lies at the
heart of who we are, it feels as if we are being torn apart
inside. But it's not just extreme cases of lost identity that
feel this; I am convinced that we all know or have known
a profound and essential loss; we are all familiar with
being lost from ourselves. At the bottom of the pile we
are all much the same, there aren't that many stories, and
not being recognised, even by ourselves, is a common
enough tale.

So all manner of ill-educated guesswork was
projected onto me, and to help make sure I wasn't seen
for what I was, I firmed up my image of being something
I wasn't. I'm not the only person in this world to do this,
in fact there are few of us who don't create an image, one
of those masks that interact with other masks, and so we
often dance our lives away without ever touching at the
centre point of where we really live, in the cave of the
heart that we all share in our essential oneness. In this
sense of separation there is a tragedy, and within that
tragedy, despair.

This is not a bad thing, in the end. It's what pushes us to finding the solution, and in the end the only thing that works is within the heart, finding and recognising who we really are. It's that boy on the beach once more; the peace and presence within the distress within ourselves; who I am under who I am not. But what is the way to find ourselves?

This is where it helps to be an outsider, like me. Or like the young woman I was talking to recently who was born in England of Indian parentage, and who is uncertain about where she belongs: in both cultures, or one of them, or neither? The questions: Who am I? Where do I belong? are of the essence. Within that question is the inherent assumption that we are not who we normally think we are—if that was the case, why would we ask the question?

It seems that many of us have an experience of what is called imposter syndrome, the more successful and prominent we are, the more likely. It's the nagging doubt that even though to everyone else you seem successful and capable, confident of yourself, at some level you are convinced that you're just bluffing your way through and that any moment now you'll be found out. Who am I? What is real? What is this game I'm playing?

The whole business of life, if you look at it like that, starts to look a bit thin and shaky. I bet I'm not the only one who has had a wave of uncertainty pass over me, not

just over my visible role, but deeper than that, as if for a
moment the whole foundation of my existence on earth
wobbled. Is this life and person I am living for real? For a
short while it seemed as if all of my life was no more than
a projection on a screen, with nothing solid and sure to
call my own. Quick, grasp for a straw! Pinch yourself,
remember your name, your story, the dramas, the
unfulfilled me, and all will be well, for a while.

Now one of the advantages of living a life like mine,
which means going deep into myself and who and what I
am, finding out, then acting on what I find no matter what
the cost, is that I had to completely dissolve the persona I
shaped and lived, into where it came from, like sugar in
tea. Then I needed to create another identity—because
we need one in this world, you can't drive a car, have a
bank account, travel to Spain without one. So I created
Persia West. As I wrote earlier, it was a bit like designing
a garden, yet another art project, wondering how bold I
could be, trusting in my inner eye and following my
heart. At least I had the assurance of being proclaimed an
artist, had faith in that eye of mine, and knew the place
from which gardens and identities are made way down in
the heart of me. So I set to creating another persona, a
fresh me, one that suited me better than the one I made
previously, which had been constructed, like most
peoples', for the satisfaction of others.

That first persona was shaped by other people's expectations, mentally-held concepts of what I should be, and into which I fitted myself, as into a mould. We all do this, of course. The trouble is that we get to think it's all true, and the shape we make ourselves into is reality, fixed, concrete, the way it is, whereas it's all just made up, a construct, out of attitudes and feelings, ideas, and other phantasms of mindstuff.

So when I let go of my identity from the baseline upwards, I found it wasn't real, fixed or concrete at all. It was made out of thin air, thoughts, convictions, assumptions and so on, which are nothing but consciousness in shapes, ephemeral and nothing much, unless we believe in them, hold on to them for dear life.

To my great interest, as the first identity crashed, I was still there, watching the demolition with horror. I felt naked, unprotected, without a skin almost, open to the elements, open to people seeing me defenceless as I emerged from the inner sea of my own consciousness. There's nothing new in this. In Greek mythology, the Goddess Aphrodite's story is similar to mine, as I am similar to her. She emerged from a mass of foam on the sea, fully formed, as a kind of transfiguration of the male genitals of the god of the Sky, Ouranos. The sea, or the ocean, is an archetypal image of the subconscious, from which all of our identities, longings, fears, powers and

identities emerge, and in the end there's no other place
to go to find ourselves.

Re-creating myself, then, was not so different from
creating the garden I can see from here as I write, the
heart-shaped pool at an angle to the house, the great
rocks, the fire over the water, the shrine to the Goddess
with its triple spirals and triumphant spires reaching into
the sky.

Almost nobody had seen what lay in my depths,
who I was that I re-made myself into, although some had.
The look in the eye of those who saw the feminine me,
was different from most eyes that saw me, or what they
thought was me. These were the people who knew who
they were themselves, so they looked directly out of
themselves without deflection, not seeing what they
wanted to see, but seeing what there was. How hard it
was for me to see myself too, because I too looked and
saw through a lens tinted with guilt and shame and
confusion, which bent and twisted simple reality and
made a world that hurt.

What terror there is, and what beauty, in making
the choice to see our own true self, not through a glass
darkly, as it says in the Bible, but directly, face to face.

25
With Grace

When I was lost in my mind, believing its stories of loneliness, bad luck, that I was a gaijin of life, an outsider who would never belong, that masculinity was an imposition for a lifetime, like a prison sentence, and all the other tales of woe that I've given you tastes of, I was not free. I was lost in the dark woods of my mind. Belief in all the stories of what I was, who I was, what was possible for me and what was not, came before the manifestation of them, the evidence of their validity, in my life. Seems to me that most of us think that what we see out there in our lives gives us the story to believe in— this is one of the cultural stories we share—but for myself in my own life, I've come to realise it's the other way round, as I've read so many times by those who've been down this road before me. You want to know what's in your mind? Look at your world. How many times have I read or heard this in my long life? How long did it take me to make it my reality?

Once upon a time on a beach in paradise I was in hell. Such is the power of the fabulous mind, and it's awesome in power: *my maya,* says Lord Krishna. The mind, I was taught, is a spark of the Self, it is just another form of consciousness, and because it too is divine in nature, it has the same inherent power to create worlds.

Then, for the boy on the beach, in an instant the whole tale vanished. It was no more than a bubble, despite its appalling power. In no time at all, literally, hell turned into heaven. My state of mind, the level of consciousness I was in, shifted from agony while lost in the wheels of the mind to utter peace, clarity, certainty, ease, in a state of no mind at all. I was out of my mind, into my heart. Joy replaced misery, certainty replaced confusion, simplicity replaced a complexity of thought.

Over the years I've wondered what happened, what made the difference on that morning that set the course of my life, and brought me here, the woman in the hills writing all this. What I have come to is that it was an act of Grace. Why I should have merited this is beyond me, but in truth the why's of life mostly are outside my understanding. In fact I no longer look for understanding, it just gets in the way of being aware, being here. Why bother with the illusion of understanding when I can be electrically present in this bright-lit moment without the need to understand anything?

How can we encourage grace, the eternal transformative force? With our own grace, is the answer, by being full of grace ourselves. Grace is a divine force which opens up the mysteries. In India, there is an image of Shiva called Nataraj, the lord of the dance. Shiva is standing on one foot, his other raised, with three arms in different postures, and the whole within a circle of fire. His limbs symbolise the five functions of the divine within us; creation, sustenance, dissolution, concealment and grace.

All these functions we live ourselves in our own everydays. I begin to write, I write, I finish writing. Just now I made breakfast, I ate breakfast, I ended breakfast. What created me, where did I come from, what supports me to exist in this life; grace? How come I don't know about this; it's not easily visible, it's concealed. How can I reveal that which is hidden? Take away that which hides, and what hides ourselves from ourselves is our mind. How is this attained? With Grace.

So awareness is everything for me. I can deal with my mind if I am aware of my mind, and once aware of its games I no longer want to play them. Move into awareness and our state of mind shifts. As my state shifts, the world transforms. Willingness, interest in doing this is my own grace.

When we disengage from believing in the unending tales of our own minds, when we dissolve our attachments to the darker tales, and then begin to have a taste for life without drama and pain, when we realise that we do exist without dark drama to define us, not only are we at peace, but magic happens.

The world carries on turning without my input. Up here in the hills of Wales it is early morning paradise, the sun came up early, very early, without asking my permission; we are days from the summer solstice, when the sun begins its track back to its winter turning. It's all delightful illusion, of course; it's us and our world that turns, not the sun. So here I am, alone in nirvana, full to bursting with all that I am. I know now that not only do I not control the greater world, I also have no need to control my own. Hands off the wheel, Persia, in fact there is no car, there is no road, there is nowhere to go but here.

The mystery, of course, is how to return to what we are, which is the story of my life, all I am writing about. How do I get back to the beach in Formentera, which is not a beach at all but a state of mind, a state of consciousness that, at some level, in some way which is our own way, we all know of in our heart of hearts?

Perhaps the essential quality for gaining the return

to what we all are, looking back on my own life, is that we want to be free more than we want to play the games of the mind. Unless we really want to, we won't do it. The constant focus on the mind, the mad belief in its dramas, as if we are the actors gone mad on the stage of life, believing not that I am an actor but I am Hamlet, I am, and the pain is all mine. Oh me, oh my, to be or not to be? Oh, to be, just to be, there is no more.

This is the most beautiful insight of all. When we move into our highest, when we become aware and conscious, when we are present, here and now, then the world works for us and with us. My vision changed; no longer am I a separate individual working hard in a tough world, now it appears that there is no separation, that was just an illusion of a contracted mind, the story upon which the stories were founded. All there is, is me.

Then, right here, in this very moment I am living, which will not always be so outwardly sweet as here in this pristine June morning, with the roaring green hills with a voice of pure divine birdsong, is my constant choice. Do I have what I want, or want what I have? This is the ultimate freedom. I want what I have, whatever it might be, I am here and now.

This is my own grace to myself, and from this my world emerges. This is the magic. Moving out of, ceasing to believe in, or stilling the mind, whatever way you like to consider it or do it, moving into that astonishing grace of presence, being, is what I looked for all my life. This is what they call the Self, who I am beyond and behind all the fantasy.

At that moment I went into the garden and took some young kale plants out of the poly-tunnel to plant out this morning. The brilliant red poppies, the big blousy oriental ones, are bursting out now in outrageous colour in this garden of subtle greens, like drag queens at the vicarage tea party. What a world!

It's not hard to be expanded, open and free, here amongst all this beauty. I know that the season I am in will change; by the next solstice the days will be very short up here in the north, it'll be gloomy and wet and cold, the leaves will be off the trees and the poppies will have retreated into the ground. But I will stay in the present, this is my commitment, because I know that every time will be the best of times when I am open and acutely aware. It will be time to keep the little wood burning stove alight, cook warm stews and plan the garden for the year ahead; perhaps, I won't know till I get there.

So with an open, expanded mind, not only do we relish what we have, but what we have changes. This is the meaning of the last lines of the verse from the Tao te Ching that set the tone for my life:

*The world is ruled by letting things take their
course, not by interfering.*

This is the genius of the aware mind. When we no
longer wander in the dark woods of our thoughts and
stories, we no longer feel the need to control our worlds.
It does just fine without our hands on the wheel—as I
wrote before; who's driving this life? Not me, I hope, I
did that and it was both tough and didn't work well. My
plans were mostly ineffective. Which reminds me of the
old Jewish joke: 'How do you make God laugh? By telling
him your plans.' Life just does what it does anyway, the
hand of God, or whatever you want to call it, does
everything, if only we don't get in the way.

When I am acutely, ecstatically, heart-fully
immediate, more magic happens. Every person in this
world wants to be in their own hearts, present and at
peace. So if we hold ourselves in our own being, they sense
and know this resonance and, as it's a heart-longing,
open up—if only for a while, but it's never forgotten. All
of us have tasted this, and at some level, none of us has
forgotten. This is our grace, our gift to everyone else, by
being in the best way of being we possibly can, by being
free we help others to be free. The spiral spirals up.

That's not all for grace. I looked in the dictionary
for the meanings of the word, and this is what came up:

elegance, beauty, and smoothness of form or movement; dignified, polite, and decent behaviour; generosity of spirit: a capacity to tolerate, accommodate, or forgive people.

These are the natural ways of being that come with awareness, openness of mind, being in the heart, being in the Self. But they not only come from being in the Self, they lead us to the Self. Become acutely conscious of the body and it will move with grace, with beauty and smoothness of movement; become acutely conscious of other people and we naturally become polite, respectful, compassionate, decent, honest. We also, without even trying, expand our capacity for tolerance and forgiveness.

A delightful twist on this is that it works the other way round. If I consciously practise being elegant, polite, respectful, forgiving, honest, and compassionate, my consciousness opens and I am expanded.

In the beginning, and in the end, if I ask myself the question in any moment of my life, at that eternal fork of choice between high road and low road: 'What is the way to go from here?', the answer is, always: go with Grace.

Lightning Source UK Ltd.
Milton Keynes UK
UKOW07f0245291214

243667UK00009B/195/P

9 780957 277502